T0301534

HERITAGE DISCOURSES IN EUROPE

COLLECTION DEVELOPMENT, CULTURAL HERITAGE, AND DIGITAL HUMANITIES

This exciting series publishes both monographs and edited thematic collections in the broad areas of cultural heritage, digital humanities, collecting and collections, public history and allied areas of applied humanities. The aim is to illustrate the impact of humanities research and in particular reflect the exciting new networks developing between researchers and the cultural sector, including archives, libraries and museums, media and the arts, cultural memory and heritage institutions, festivals and tourism, and public history.

HERITAGE DISCOURSES IN EUROPE

RESPONDING TO MIGRATION, MOBILITY, AND CULTURAL IDENTITIES IN THE TWENTY-FIRST CENTURY

Edited by
LAIA COLOMER AND ANNA CATALANI

We dedicate this book to our parents:
Renato Catalani *(1936–2018)*

and

Pilar Solsona *(1942–2019),*
who taught us to be resilient and
determined in every endeavour.

British Library Cataloguing in Publication Data
A catalogue record for this book is available from the British Library

© 2020, Arc Humanities Press, Leeds

ISBN: 9781641892025
e-ISBN: 9781641892032

www.arc-humanities.org
Printed and bound in the UK (by CPI Group [UK] Ltd), USA (by Bookmasters), and elsewhere using print-on-demand technology.

CONTENTS

Chapter 1. Cultural Identities, Migration, and Heritage in Contemporary
  Europe: An Introduction 1
  LAIA COLOMER and ANNA CATALANI

Chapter 2. Narratives of Resilient Heritage and the "Capacity to Aspire"
  during Displacement. 11
  ANNA CATALANI

Chapter 3. Museum Theatre, Refugee Artists, Contingent Identities,
  and Heritage 25
  ALISON JEFFERS

Chapter 4. Museums, Activism, and the "Ethics of Care": Two Museum
  Exhibitions on the Refugee "Crisis" in Greece in 2016. 39
  ALEXANDRA BOUNIA

Chapter 5. Heritage Education from the Ground: Historic Schools, Cultural
  Diversity, and Sense of Belonging in Barcelona 53
  MARIA FELIU-TORRUELLA, PALOMA GONZÁLEZ-MARCÉN, and
  CLARA MASRIERA-ESQUERRA

Chapter 6. Heritage Processes following Relocation: The Russian Old
  Believers of Romania 69
  CRISTINA CLOPOT

Chapter 7. Doing Things/Things Doing: Mobility, Things, Humans,
  Home, and the Affectivity of Migration 83
  LAIA COLOMER-SOLSONA

Chapter 8. Staging Musical Heritage in Europe through Continuity
  and Change. 99
  AMANDA BRANDELLERO

Afterword. Superdiversity and New Approaches to Heritage and Identities in
   Europe: The Way Forward 111
   SOPHIA LABADI

Index..117

Illustrations

Figure 4.1. "A Museum without a Home" exhibition poster as displayed on
   one of the metro trains in Athens.....................................45

Figure 5.1. Building of the Pere Vila primary school, architect Josep Goday. 58

Figure 5.2. Building of the Menendez Pelayo secondary school, architect
   Josep Mestres..58

Figure 5.3. Children of the Àngel Baixeras primary school examining the school
   notebooks of the first pupils of the 1930s.............................61

Figure 5.4. Students of the Menéndez Pelayo secondary school during field
   research in the neighbourhood..63

Figure 6.1. Religious service for the blessing of the fruits. 74

Figure 6.2. Men reading in Slavonic during the Christmas service. 76

Figure 7.1. Travelling salvaged objects moving along with Abdi-Noor
   Mohamed's family, and posted by him at *The Archaeology of a Mobile
   Life* Facebook group...88

Figure 7.2. Travelling salvaged object moving along with Paloma González
   Marcén, and posted by her at *The Archaeology of a Mobile Life*
   Facebook group...90

Figure 7.3. Travelling salvaged object moving along with Amy Clare Tasker,
   and posted by her at *The Archaeology of a Mobile Life*
   Facebook group...92

Chapter 1

CULTURAL IDENTITIES, MIGRATION, AND HERITAGE IN CONTEMPORARY EUROPE: AN INTRODUCTION

LAIA COLOMER and ANNA CATALANI

THIS VOLUME CONSISTS of seven chapters and one afterword by leading and up-and-coming academics who work on cultural identity and heritage. Significant research has already been done in the field of heritage studies highlighting, for example, meanings, experiences, and discourses in heritage, history, and nationalism, diaspora and migration, and cosmopolitanism and globalization.[1] The aim of this volume is to expand on this by analyzing the role of cultural heritage and by especially focusing on the intersection between identity, memory, mobilities, and sociocultural agency.

Underpinned by neoliberal orthodoxies, today's matters—such as population flows, economic dynamics, environmental changes, and media politics—are becoming worldwide concerns that can no longer be managed and addressed solely within a national context. In order to avoid perpetuating postcolonial inequalities and unsustainable environmental circumstances, these issues require a "glocal" approach, that is to say, both a global and a local modus operandi. This glocal perspective offers new scenarios with regards to cultural representations, cultural heritage, and identity formation. Most nation-state discourses, indeed, no longer offer people a clear guide to understanding who belongs together and in what way they relate to each other.[2] A lack of solid narratives about social belonging drives groups and individuals either to look for security in traditional cultural discourses of identity (that only reinforce old narratives of "we," "home/homeland," and "the other")[3] or to explore new forms of cultural identity in solidarity (that in turn generate other forms of togetherness and engagement in the community). Both discourses and new forms of cultural identity, though, are not necessarily defined by citizenship, passports, or geographical origins and hence are more fluid in their characterization, shaping, and understanding.[4]

According to the Office of the United Nations High Commissioner for Refugees (UNHCR), the world is facing the highest level of displacement ever experienced, with an unprecedented 65.3 million people forced from their homes because of war, internal

---

1 For an overview of the most relevant works produced in these fields in the past decades, see Anheier and Isar, *Heritage, Memory and Identity*; Waterton and Watson, *Palgrave Handbook*; Fairclough, Jameson, and Schofield, *Heritage Reader*; Logan, Nic Craith, and Kockel, *A Companion*; Labrador and Silberman, *Oxford Handbook*.

2 Schierup, Hansen, and Castles, *Migration, Citizenship*.

3 Betz, "Against Globalization."

4 Castells, "Globalisation and Identity."

conflicts, environmental crises, or poor economies. Amongst these, 21.3 million are refugees; the rest are economic migrants and internally displaced persons.[5] During the past four years, Europe has also been affected by such mass movements, with refugees and displaced people coming from Asia, Africa, and the Middle East. Since then, these mass movements have become known as the "2015 refugee crises." However, this is only one example of the large-scale displacements that are nowadays taking place across the globe and that are creating, in a postcolonial context, new forms of cultural creolization or hybridization.[6] Compared with previous displacements and the resulting sociocultural interactions, these new encounters are marked and influenced by the effects of globalization and hence it is important to briefly define our understanding of globalization in contemporary Europe.

Globalization, it can be argued, is currently defined by trans-planetary and supra-territorial connectivities, understood as social and cultural links between people located anywhere across the globe.[7] These connectivities operate next to and are mixed with those based on physical proximity (e.g., neighbourhood and local community).[8] Consequently people's cultural identities are created and negotiated not only in local contexts, but also within the international scene, by retaining links with other cultures or societies of origins (e.g., in the case of migrants and diasporic groups)[9] and through the means of digital and social media. Hence, it is possible to say that more people than before live in spaces/places that are not exclusively nation-bound but that are both local *and* global arenas. Papastergiadis[10] uses the phrase "deterritorialisation of culture" to refer to the ways in which cultural formation is no longer linked to physical proximity to a given cultural centre. Instead the term defines people's capacity to demarcate their cultural identity and community belonging in different sociocultural landscapes—or "global ethnoscapes."[11] Within this scenario, migrants (both forced and not) are not just the subjects of policies of integration, neither are they simply a workforce in, debatably, welcoming societies. They are sociocultural contributors who take action, make decisions, and create social relations both in the country of origin and in the country of settlement.[12] These interactions generate new forms of cultural creolization and have direct consequences on the ways in which cultural heritage is defined and gains significance amongst groups, both local and glocal.[13] This book aims to explore exactly this ongoing challenge and the resulting discourses about cultural heritage and identity in contemporary Europe.

Europe and its cultural heritage, it is fair to say, have changed markedly in comparison to a decade ago. Today's cultural, economic, and historical changes are also having

5 UNHCR, "Figures at a Glance."
6 Bhabha, "The Third Space"; Pieterse, *Globalization and Culture.*
7 Tomlinson, "Globalization and Cultural Identity."
8 Scholte, *Globalization.*
9 Glick Schiller, "A Global Perspective"; Vertovec, *Transnationalism.*
10 Papastergiadis, *Turbulence of Migration.*
11 Appadurai, *Modernity at Large.*
12 Glick Schiller, "Explanatory Frameworks."
13 Colomer, "Heritage on the Move."

an impact on the understanding and shaping of European heritage.[14] Additionally, in line with the globalization effect, the once-familiar "European cultural dimension" has been transforming from defined nations and clear, national cultural identities to a cultural mosaic, where entangled traditions, narratives, and identities are redefining a new cultural landscape.[15] Key catalysts have been, as we have said, the migratory movements, whether voluntary (e.g., work, affective liaisons, family reunifications, studies, retirement, social freedom, and career trajectory) or forced (e.g., war, climate change, political/gender persecution). However, it is important to specify that although migration has been traditionally understood as merely performed by people from outside Europe, reaching European shores due to economic reasons conflict, within this volume, we intend to widen this notion and include all kinds of mobilities occurring and transforming our understanding of the humanity living in Europe. This is because alongside Senegalese, Ecuadorian, Iraqi, Pakistan, Chinese, and Turkish immigration, Europe displays important ethnic variations at the level of internal migration, with a clear geographical gradient with high mobility in Northern and Western Europe but lower mobility in Southern and Eastern Europe.[16] Internal European Union (EU) migration responds to housing markets, financial deregulation, economic growth, the labour market, health facilities, and higher education exchange facilities, and includes an increasing number of young adults, retired citizens, intercultural families, and single women.

Based on these reflections, our starting point is that the human geography of Europe today is much more complex and radically different to the one of even a decade ago: it is made by a number of geographies and ethnicities, which generate and negotiate the merging of new identities and cultural narratives, differently from those assumed by the traditional socio-ontology of methodological nationalism.[17] Therefore this volume aims to explore closely these new expressions and negotiations of cultural identities, focusing on the uses and significance of European cultural heritage today, as well as the discourses generated about it. The core questions the contributors address dwell on cultural identities in transformation and in relation to heritage (or its absence) but also on the ways in which cultural organizations and heritage sites become meeting points for discussions, creative exchanges, and development between the different cultures shaping Europe today. Specifically, the authors question how new cultural identities are challenging the notions and significance of cultural heritage during the era of forced migration and mass movements; they consider the ways in which the current authorized heritage discourses in Europe are changing because of migration and globalization as well as the extent heritage sites and museums that can become effective meeting points for socio-cultural dialogues between locals and newcomers. Finally, this volume's authors have also been exploring the ways in which heritage sites can be creative platforms for heritage discourses, better "tuned" to today's European multicultural profile and thereby better reflecting current European reality.

---

14 Harrison, *Heritage*; Smith, *Uses of Heritage*.

15 Delanty, "Entangled Memories."

16 Bernard, "Cohort Measures of Internal Migration."

17 Beck, "The Cosmopolitan State."

Outline of the Chapters

This book fits within a fast-growing body of research and academic literature examining the complex phenomena of migration and cultural heritage.[18] It aims to make, though, a unique contribution to the topic by focusing on the different and interlaced narratives of cultural heritage, identity, migration, and mobility, and by contextualizing them within the multifaceted context of contemporary Europe. Past and recent work on the subject area has mainly considered how cultural institutions have approached and represented migration in Europe, and how mobility has been challenging the society and contribution of museums and heritage sites towards the understanding of migratory experiences.[19] Furthermore, research on museum displays has shown how exhibitions dealing with migration have included primarily benign representations of migrants and their material culture. Although such displays have aimed to engage, through participatory approaches, with the migrant minorities, they remain Western-centred interpretations, whereby migrants and refugees are seemingly presented as people in need of humanitarian intervention and support. Additionally, a growing body of literature has also been looking at museums and their social responsibility in relation to minority groups and with regards to prejudice, equality, social justice, and citizenship.[20] Such work has highlighted the need "to differentiate between performative activism and operational activism," with the former being a just a "show" rather than a real engagement with the people represented.[21]

The chapters included in this volume build on this work and question further the changes that heritage, as a concept, as a practice, and as a performance,[22] is going through due to the cultural clashes and/or opportunities for cultural regeneration (of individuals and groups) created by mobilities and migrations in contemporary Europe. It questions, through different case studies and perspectives, the role that individuals, as the hosts of the welcoming country or as the newcomers, have in shaping heritage in contemporary Europe.[23] Cultural heritage here is understood as an action, as a process through which cultural identities are revealed, questioned, negotiated, and (re)created, rather than acting only as a mirror of past identities. The chapters included in this volume thus explore this unfolding situation, taking a wide understanding of cultural heritage, stemming from museum studies, memory studies, public archaeology, and ethnography and dealing with a variety of contingent issues, such as education, museum performance, affect, and care, intangible heritage and the idea of absence, musical heritage, religious practices

---

18 Levin, *Global Mobilities*; Gouriévidis, *Museums and Migration*; Whitehead, Lloyd, Eckersley, and Mason, *Museums, Migration and Identity*; Innocenti, *Cultural Networks*; Ang, "Unsettling the National"; Amescua, "Anthropology of Intangible Cultural Heritage and Migration."

19 Macdonald, *Museum, National, Postnational*; Bounia, Nikiforidou, Nikonanou, and Matossian, *Voices from the Museum*; Hegardt, *Museum Beyond.*

20 Sandell and Nightingale, *Museums, Equality and Social Justice*; Message, *Museums and Racism*; Labadi, *Museums, Immigrants, and Social Justice.*

21 From a conversation between Alisdair Hudson and Bernadette Lynch, quoted in Lynch, "'I'm gonna do something.' Moving beyond Talk in the Museum."

22 Haldrup and Bærenholdt, "Heritage as Performance."

23 Nettleford, "Migration, Transmission and Maintenance."

in a globalized world, and human–thing entanglements. These inter- and cross-disciplinary perspectives complement each other and show the necessity of a diversity of approaches, as a key methodology, to understand the complexity of today's cultural heritage and identity in Europe, particularly with respect to mobility and globalization.

This volume comprises seven chapters, whose authors are all female academics from different disciplines, different European countries, and at different stages of their careers. While this was not intentional, it is a welcome coincidence in the current social and cultural climate. The book starts with an exploration of the relationship between intangible cultural heritage and cultural identities in Europe, from the point of view of refugees and forced migrants. In her chapter, Anna Catalani dwells on the notion of the absence of intangible cultural heritage during displacement. Catalani considers the binomial absence–presence of heritage as a staged process, starting from the assumption that human beings experience absence as an emotional, temporary rupture with their cultural traditions. This rupture develops through three phases: from an initial lack of intangible heritage (which means "putting aside" the known cultural traditions to focus on the journey); to an "absent presence" of heritage, where cultural heritage becomes the object of longing, through selected memories; to a re-acknowledged presence of heritage, through a redefinition of cultural traditions in the new context. This latter phase takes place only when the temporary disconnection between displaced individuals and their heritage has been elaborated and the felt absence of intangible heritage can become a catalyst for positive personal and collective changes as well as for identity redefinition.

Alison Jeffers returns to issues on the complexity of refugee artists' identity and how this complexity could be explored in museum performances. In her contribution, she looks at the complexities of being a "refugee artist" in a heritage setting and at the emerging potential value of conceptualizing heritage and identity as contingent. Theatre performance, though, is here being acted out within museum institutions, thereby using colonial cultural heritage "deposited" in British museums, as a means of both challenging and destabilizing contingent identities, either of the refugees and "their heritage" in the museums or those of their audience as members of a local community. Performing a multiplicity of heritages is a way of narrating the multiplicity of identities, of both refugee artists and local audiences, and of the heritage they engage with, in today's postcolonial institutions/refugee "crisis."

Alexandra Bounia's chapter further explores issues of heritage and the so-called refugee crisis in Europe, this time focusing on the social responsibility of museums as activist institutions. Following the work of Schellenbacher and Message, Bounia considers the ways in which museums can respond to the traumatic and complicated phenomenon of migration, by going beyond their role as "social mirrors" of past events (e.g., narratives of the migration/refugee phenomena) and instead becoming creators of new cultural agendas and agencies, like combating social injustices and becoming promoters of new social community relations in terms of solidarity, responsibility, trust, and human rights. For that, she draws on the feminist political theory of the "ethics of care." This ethics of care provides an interesting lens through which to analyze works Greek museums undertook in 2016 in order to develop relationships of care between people touched by the refugee "crisis," and reflect on how these institutions could move towards redefining their role as agents of care in an age of mobility, globalization, and neoliberalism.

School education probably focuses more on the ethics of care of future citizens than on exclusively transmitting knowledge. Maria Feliu-Torruella, Paloma González-Marcén, and Clara Masriera-Esquerra's chapter explores heritage education as a key political tool for civic values fostering tolerance, social integration, and citizenship between pupils and families of different cultural backgrounds and origins, using critical issues of cultural heritage such as diversity, cultural rights, and peaceful and democratic coexistence. Accordingly, heritage here is not something that we inherit from the past to be appreciated and enjoyed, but an expression of rights and values that must be acknowledged, negotiated, and reappropriated, democratically, today. Agency-oriented heritage projects, developed in schools like the examples introduced by these authors, can become a critical practice for citizenship education in Europe by exploring questions of what kind of society we want in the future rather than narrating where we come from culturally.

Issues of identity, roots, and routes are explored in detail by Cristina Clopot and Laia Colomer: the former from a diaspora and religious perspective; the latter exploring notions of homing and belonging. Clopot analyzes the heritage narratives of Russian Old Believers of Romania as a process to resist change in the age of globalization and transmigration. Colomer analyzes narratives of affect towards travelling salvaged objects amongst different type of migrants. Both, though, focus on the apparent contradiction between places and flows as key elements in identity processes amongst today's old and new Europeans. Clopot's focal points are "ethnic group" cultures, their efforts towards heritage preservation (even though the group is disseminated throughout Europe), and how these narratives reflect or refract a European ethos on localism, nationalism, multiculturalism, and cosmopolitanism (e.g., whether they are "united in diversity"). Colomer's chapter, instead, spotlights the entanglement between migrants and those objects selected on purpose to be companions in mobility, and therefore how they act as embodied emotional memories of past, present, and future lives. Throughout this exploration Colomer seeks to define the ways in which such relationships can provide new forms of museum display that exhibit the material culture accompanying mobile subjects.

Finally, Amanda Brandellero's chapter examines the staging of folk music as a perfect metaphor of intercultural processes occurring in Europe. The chapter draws from the experience of programmers and performers of world music festivals in Europe. Their activity engages directly with the diversity of musical genres and cultural expressions, its consuming tendencies, and the resulting creolization in musical creativity. Brandellero argues that their practice as music promoters, producers, and practitioners is an active exploration both of music as a meaningful practice of intangible heritage—against the backdrop of today's European cultural diversity—and of the ways in which this active process of musical production results in recognizing, legitimating, constructing, dissenting, and discarding different cultural identities inside Europe.

Both cultural heritage and cultural identity are characterized by a broad range of meanings ascribed to them. This is because their dynamic nature is part of a constant process of collective and individual creation, negotiation, and creolization. This book explores these dimensions in Europe, taking into account powerful forces of mobility in today's globalized world. While this book is not a complete compendium of the ongoing, changing, and multiple heritage discourses in Europe on cultural heritage and identity, it aims to grasp some of their essential aspects. Hence, by acknowledging that any experience of movement produces novel forms of belonging and identity, while stimulating shifts in the understanding of cultural heritage, this volume intends to trigger critical reflections on different, ongoing discourses developing right now in Europe about heritage and identity. Such discourses shape and contribute in different ways to the human geography of an inclusive Europe.

Bibliography

Amescua, Cristina. "Anthropology of Intangible Cultural Heritage and Migration: An Unchartered Field." In *Anthropological Perspectives on Intangible Cultural Heritage*. Edited by Lourdes Arizpe and Cristina Amescua, 103–20. New York: Springer, 2013.

Ang, Ian. "Unsettling the National: Heritage and Diaspora." In *Heritage, Memory and Identity*. Edited by Helmut Anheier and Yudhishthir Raj Isar, 82–94. London: Sage, 2011.

Anheier, Helmut, and Yudhishthir Raj Isar. *Heritage, Memory and Identity*. London: Sage, 2011.

Appadurai, Arjun, *Modernity at Large: Cultural Dimensions of Globalization.* Minneapolis: University of Minnesota Press, 1996.

Beck, Ulrich. "The Cosmopolitan State: Redefining Power in the Global Age." *International Journal of Cultural Sociology* 181 (2005): 143–59.

Bernard, Aude. "Cohort Measures of Internal Migrations: Understanding Long-Term Trends." *Demography* 54 (2017): 2201–21.

Betz, Hans-Georg. "Against Globalization: Xenophobia, Identity Politics and Exclusionary Populism in Western Europe." In *Fighting Identities: Race, Religion and Ethno-nationalism*. Edited by Leo Panitch and Colin Leys, 193–210. Merlin: London, 2002.

Bhahba, Homi K. "The Third Space. Interview with Homi Bhahba." In *Identity: Community, Culture, Difference*. Edited by Jonathan Rutherford, 207–21. London: Lawrence & Wishart, 1990.

Bounia, Alexandra, Alexandra Nikiforidou, Niki Nikonanou, and Albert Dicran Matossian. *Voices from the Museum: Survey Research in Europe's National Museums*. EuNaMus Report 5. Linköping: Linköping University Electronic Press, 2012.

Castells, Manuel. "Globalisation and Identity: A Comparative Perspective." *Transfer* 1 (2006): 56–67.

Colomer, Laia. "Heritage on the Move: Cross-Cultural Heritage as a Response to Globalisation, Mobilities and Multiple Migrations." *International Journal of Heritage Studies* 23 (2017): 913–27.

Delanty, Gerard. "Entangled Memories: How to Study Europe's Cultural Heritage. *European Legacy* 22 (2017): 129–45.

Fairclough, Graham, John H. Jameson Jr., and John Schofield, eds. *The Heritage Reader*. London: Routledge, 2008.

Glick Schiller, Nina. "Explanatory Frameworks in Transnational Migration Studies: The Missing Multi-scalar Global Perspective." *Ethnic and Racial Studies* 38 (2015): 2275–82.

——. "A Global Perspective on Transnational Migration: Theorizing Migration without Methodological Nationalism." In *Diaspora and Transnationalism: Concepts, Theories and Methods*. Edited by Rainer Bauböck and Thomas Faist, 109–29. Amsterdam: Amsterdam University Press, 2010.

Gouriévidis, Laurence. *Museums and Migration: History, Memory and Politics.* London: Routledge, 2014.

Haldrup, Michael, and Jørgen Ole Bærenholdt. "Heritage as Performance." In *The Palgrave Handbook of Contemporary Heritage Research.* Edited by Emma Waterton and Steve Watson, 52–64. Basingstoke: Palgrave Macmillan, 2015.

Harrison, Rodney. *Heritage: Critical Approaches.* London: Routledge, 2013.

Hegardt, Johan. *The Museum beyond the Nation.* Stockholm: National Historical Museum, 2012.

Innocenti, Perla. *Cultural Connectors in Migrating Heritage: Intersecting Theories and Practices across Europe.* Farnham: Ashgate, 2015.

Labadi, Sophia. *Museums, Immigrants, and Social Justice.* London: Routledge, 2018.

Labrador, Angela, and Neil Silberman, eds. *The Oxford Handbook of Public Heritage Theory and Practice.* Oxford: Oxford University Press, 2018.

Levin, Amy. *Global Mobilities: Refugees, Exiles, and Immigration Museums and Archives.* London: Routledge, 2017.

Logan, William, Máiréad Nic Craith, and Ullrich Kockel, eds. *A Companion to Heritage Studies.* Chichester: Wiley, 2016.

Lynch, Bernadette. "'I'm gonna do something.' Moving beyond Talk in the Museum." In *Museum Activism.* Edited by Robert R. Janes and Richard Sandell, 114–30. New York: Routledge, 2019.

Macdonald, Sharon J. "Museum, National, Postnational and Transcultural Identities." *Museum and Society* 1 (2003): 1–16.

Message, Kylie. *Museums and Racism.* Abingdon: Routledge, 2018.

Nettleford, Rex. "Migration, Transmission and Maintenance of the Intangible Heritage." *Museum International* 56 (2004): 78–83.

Papastergiadis, Nikos. *The Turbulence of Migration: Globalization, Deterritorialization and Hybridity.* Oxford: Polity, 2000.

Pieterse, Jan Nederveen. *Globalization and Culture: Global Mélange.* Lanham: Rowman & Littlefield, 2004.

Sandell, Richard, and Eithne Nightingale. *Museums, Equality and Social Justice.* London: Routledge, 2012.

Schierup, Carl-Ulrik, Peo Hansen, and Stephen Castles. *Migration, Citizenship and the European Welfare State: A European Dilemma.* Oxford: Oxford University Press, 2006.

Scholte, Jan Aart. *Globalization: A Critical Introduction.* Basingstoke: Palgrave Macmillan, 2005.

Smith, Laurajane, *Uses of Heritage.* London: Routledge, 2006.

Stefano, Michelle L., and Peter Davis. *Routledge Companion to Intangible Cultural Heritage.* London: Routledge, 2017.

Tomlinson, John. "Globalization and Cultural Identity." In *The Global Transformations Reader: An Introduction to the Globalization Debate.* Edited by David Held and Anthony McGrew, 269–77. London: Polity, 2003.

UNHCR. "Figures at a Glance." www.unhcr.org/figures-at-a-glance.html. Retrieved February 5, 2019.

Vertovec, Steven. 2009. *Transnationalism.* London: Routledge, 2009.

Waterton, Emma, and Steve Watson. *The Palgrave Handbook of Contemporary Heritage Research.* London: Palgrave Macmillan, 2015.

Whitehead, Christopher, Katherine Lloyd, Susannah Eckersley, and Rhiannon Mason. *Museums, Migration and Identity in Europe: Peoples, Places and Identities.* Farnham: Ashgate, 2015.

Laia Colomer Norwegian Institute for Cultural Heritage Research, Norway; email: laia.colomer@niku.no. **Anna Catalani** Lincoln School of Design, University of Lincoln, United Kingdom; email: acatalani@lincoln.ac.uk.

Chapter 2

NARRATIVES OF RESILIENT HERITAGE AND THE "CAPACITY TO ASPIRE" DURING DISPLACEMENT

ANNA CATALANI

Introduction

THIS CHAPTER IS concerned with the notions of and the relationship between intangible cultural heritage and cultural identity, in relation to displaced individuals, and in the context of contemporary Europe. The starting point is that people's movements have at their heart the encounter between newcomers and local communities. These encounters translate into situated stories and new cultural discourses about resilience, which, in the longer term, are likely to contribute to the formation of a shared European heritage.[1] However, amongst newcomers, and especially those who, like refugees, experience displacement, the idea of heritage is particularly problematic, due to personal struggles with cultural and physical belonging. In order to be part, eventually, of a body of shared cultural practices, the heritage of displaced individuals needs first to "die" so that it can be revalued and rearticulated through an osmotic and yet aspirational process, generated by its perceived absence. Therefore, this chapter aims to consider exactly this, by addressing the following questions: Can we speak, at all, of an absence of (intangible) heritage during displacement? If heritage does (not) die, how is it then revalued and redefined during displacement? What cultural discourses are developing around the idea of "heritage" during forced migration?

In order to answer these questions, this chapter has been organized into four sections. In the first section, I consider the notions of displaced people and intangible cultural heritage (during displacement), the latter understood as a non-fixed concept subject to constant reinterpretations. In the second section, I explore the pairing "absence—presence" and I define it as a phased, emotional rupture with cultural traditions and heritage practices. The third section focuses on the "capacity to aspire," as defined by Arjun Appadurai,[2] and on the ways in which it triggers amongst displaced individuals, through a perceived absence of heritage, the aspiration to revaluate and rearticulate their cultural traditions. In the final section, I present some critical reflections on "resilient heritage," that is to say those forms of intangible heritage that survive trauma, which

---

1 McDowell, "Heritage, Memory and Identity"; Halbwachs, *On Collective Memory.*
2 Appadurai, *Future as Cultural Fact.*

are reshaped through selective remembering[3] and which foster a sense of cultural worth and belonging, especially in the earlier stages of resettlement.[4]

People in Displacement

In March 2017, I took part in an event organized by the Rethink Rebuild Society, a charity organization aiming to improve the lives of refugees, asylum seekers, and immigrants, in particular but not exclusively Syrians in the United Kingdom. The event (titled "Living Library—A Refugee in Manchester") was held at the Longsight Library and Learning Centre in Manchester and its purpose was to allow members of the public to meet, for about fifteen minutes, ten different people who were either refugees or who had worked in some capacity (either as artists or as social workers) with refugees. Through short chats, the public was given the opportunity to hear about precarious journeys and the resulting displacement, and to be inspired by personal stories of resilience and to reflect, together with their interlocutors, on these stories. One of the "participants" was a young refugee from the Republic of Congo. During my brief interaction with him, I was interested to find out his story and at the same time I was keen to understand what "heritage" meant to him, both before his ordeal and in his current situation. His reply, however, was not what I expected: he plainly explained that there is no heritage for a refugee. Heritage (the idea or the understanding of it) and any memory associated with it had died the moment he became a refugee. Although this was the view of one individual—and it is not possible to extend it unanimously to the broader refugee community—it made me both think about the meaning of heritage itself in relation to displacement and question whether heritage can really disappear in the context of forced movements. Already in ordinary circumstances, we cannot speak of a "fixed" idea of heritage, but rather of a changeable process which reflects the relationship we have with the past, even a recent one.[5] Heritage, hence, can be an ephemeral and even dissonant "entity" which is difficult, in specific circumstances, to acknowledge, define, or agree about.[6] For instance, its fluctuating nature is accentuated during displacement, when its embodied cultural practices, meanings, and symbols are continuously reframed, altered, and sometimes misunderstood due to the journey's unpredictability and the multiple cultural interactions.

My interlocutor's comment also triggered reflections on the "if" and "why" heritage should matter when someone is displaced. Undoubtedly, the unsettling feeling of being forced to leave home is not conducive to rejoicing. Thus, heritage is subject to continuous revaluation and renegotiation, especially when different cultures are forced to interact and ultimately clash. Current work on displacement in Europe has in fact shown that the initial response of host communities to refugees and (forced) migrants

3 Harrison, "Forgetting to Remember, Remembering to Forget."
4 Halilovich, *Places of Pain.*
5 Smith, *Uses of Heritage*; Harrison and Rose, "Intangible Heritage"; Harrison, *Heritage. Critical Approaches.*
6 Smith, "The 'Doing' of Heritage: Heritage as Performance."

is characterized by social tensions, cultural misunderstanding, and, sadly, by a rise in ideological extremism.[7] This makes it difficult to appreciate the heritage (especially in its intangible forms) of displaced individuals as well as their possible contributions to the hosting country, while it intensifies their distress and concerns.[8] Besides being physical situations, displacement and forced migration are emotional states. As refugees and forced migrants leave their homes, undertake painful journeys, and attempt to resettle in another country, they find themselves crossing physical, emotional, and cultural borders. Being "displaced" means to be tolerated guests in a new context. It means to have limited opportunities as legitimate residents and not being fully able to freely share ideas, values, and traditions.[9] The status of "guests" restricts what might have been possible and natural in the country of origin: it exposes displaced individuals to unpredictable everyday situations, whilst they attempt to redefine their lives and reassert their identities. Above all, the condition of displacement heightens the longing for familiar people, idioms, objects, and habits and exposes the painful absence of the known and familiar.[10] Forced migrants and displaced individuals are almost "imprisoned" in an in-between condition, which continuously shifts between the yearning for a known reality, the necessity to fit in the hosting country, and a melancholic awareness of the absence of "their things," places, people, rituals, and, ultimately, of their own identities.[11]

Binomial Absence–Presence as a Three-Stage Process

When speaking, in general terms, about "absence" (e.g., the absence of something or someone), the feeling of "lacking" comes in various forms, all of which have an impact on people's lives and on their perception of the self. As human beings, rather than comprehending "absence" only through the lack of materiality, we experience it, first and foremost, as an emotional rupture with something or someone.[12] This rupture causes a loss of coherence with what matters:[13] things, settings, or other people become less meaningful when their absence is experienced. This is primarily because absence is a feeling that "exists through relations" that give matter to absence itself—like, for instance, when the absence of a loved one can shape the whole atmosphere of a room or an event.[14] Hence it is possible to say that absence is oxymoronic in nature: the subject of

---

7 Lucassen, "Peeling an Onion."

8 Carling and Collins, "Aspiration, Desire and Drivers of Migration"; see also Chatelard, *Intangible Cultural Heritage of Displaced Syrians*; Nguyen, *The Displaced*.

9 This lack of opportunities and connection with local communities is aggravated by a lack of adequate language skills, especially at the beginning of the "resettlement."

10 Chatelard, *Intangible Cultural Heritage of Displaced Syrians*, 19.

11 McDowell, "Heritage, Memory and Identity."

12 Hetherington, "Secondhandedness," 159; Meyer, "Placing and Tracing Absence," 103.

13 Frers, "Confronting Absence." See also Moran and Disney, "It's a Horrible, Horrible 'Feeling'"; Degnen, "'Knowing,' Absence, and Presence."

14 Meyer, "Placing and Tracing Absence"; Felder, Duineveld, and van Assche, "Absence/Presence."

an absence (for instance, intangible cultural heritage as cultural practices during forced migration) can still be present in some ways (through memories and stories shared by members of the same group) and yet absent in others (through a lack of material culture associated with it or an impossibility to perform the rituals in a new context). Furthermore, absence is highly performative: as an "embodied phenomenon," it relies on meaningful, physical interactions between individuals and the absent object, person, or idea. As Frers explains, "based on their corporal relation to the world around them, individuals fill the hole left by absences by drawing on their own particular embodied memories and habits [...] embedded in social structures and connected to places."[15] These habits, or rather the lack of them, as recurring experiences, determine the awareness of what is missing and the need to fill the void through personal memories and reenactment of what has been missing.[16]

Taking into account these points and with regards to intangible cultural heritage during displacement, it is not helpful to conjecture about an absence of heritage but rather discuss the binomial "absence–presence," which I understand as a temporary and yet evolving emotional three-stage rupture between displaced individuals and their intangible cultural heritage.[17] Within this context, the adjective "temporary" indicates that during displacement the absence–presence of intangible cultural heritage follows almost a phased transformation, leading eventually to a fully acknowledged presence of intangible heritage. The phased transformation takes place, at the same time, with personal elaborations about displacement, geographical resettlement, and the redefinition of identity in the "there" and "then." Specifically, the absence–presence of intangible heritage evolves in the following way: from a pragmatic lack of heritage (especially in the initial phase of migration), when displaced individuals have to "put aside" their known realities and traditions and focus on the challenges of the journey; to an "absent presence" of heritage, where, although cultural heritage is still subordinated to the day-to-day taking up of resettlement information, it starts to became the object of longing (as, most likely, in the case of the Congolese refugee I met), through the selection of memories[18] about cultural traditions; to, finally, the reacknowledged and reinstated presence of such heritage, which consents a reconsideration, redefinition, and, in some cases, adaptation of such cultural traditions to the new context and as resilient links with the past. This latter phase (the "reacknowledgement of the presence") takes place when

---

15 Frers, "Confronting Absence," 287.

16 Harrison, "Beyond 'Natural' and 'Cultural' Heritage," 264.

17 Primarily as traditional practices and traditions.

18 In this chapter, I understand selective memories and remembering as an intentional act through which refugees and displaced individuals choose to forget those episodes of their past that may be too destabilizing, in favour of remembering those that can counter the narrative of the trauma of displacement. See Muzaini, "On the Matter of Forgetting and Memory Returns"; Lacroix and Fiddian-Qasmiyeh, "Refugee and Diaspora Memories"; Erll, *Memory in Culture*; Connerton, "Seven Types of Forgetting"; and Delanty, "Entangled Memories." With regards to the positive effect of autobiographical narratives, see McLean, Pasupathi, and Pals, "Selves Creating Stories Creating Selves."

the temporary disconnection between refugees and their heritage has become evident and it has been elaborated: hence the process of reconnecting with traditions can begin and also sets the basis for a shared heritage.

This chapter focuses on the second and final phases of this process, that is to say the evolution from an absent presence of heritage to a present resilient heritage. With regards to the latter point, note that the process of remembering "is not a [mere] matter of retrieving but [rather] of reshaping in a new mechanism of selection":[19] it is a selective process through which the memories of past cultural traditions become associated primarily with a sense of personal worth and can help displaced individuals to positively redefine their identity and validate their heritage in the hosting context. Therefore, the absent presence of intangible heritage during displacement becomes almost the ideal, powerful condition that triggers positive personal revaluations, cultural reinstatement, and aspirations for social transformations, activated in the final phase of this binomial relationship.

The Capacity to Aspire and Intangible Cultural Heritage

In *The Future as Cultural Fact*, Arjun Appadurai explores the idea of the capacity to aspire, an ability embedded and nurtured in the past and yet focused on future ideas and possibilities. He explains: "the future is ours to design, if we are attuned to the right risks, the right speculations and the right understanding of the material world we both inherit and shape."[20] According to Appadurai, indeed, individuals' imagination and resourcefulness are future-oriented cultural attitudes, necessary to raise from disadvantageous situations and create better futures. Although his focus is on India (and specifically on the conditions of the poor living in Mumbai slums), his argument is very much applicable to any context, whereby disadvantaged groups, like refugees, have to find the cultural resources to contest and positively alter their social and human condition numerous times and in multiple cultural and geographical contexts.[21] Hence, in relation to displacement, the interconnection between intangible cultural heritage, its absent presence, and the capacity to aspire offers a helpful framework to carry out critical and new reflections on the reasons why cultural heritage matters during hardship and how its revaluation could happen amongst displaced individuals because of its absent presence.

Work has been done on the capacity to aspire in relation to migration (primarily on the children of migrants) and the heritage sector (with regards to heritage tourism).[22]

---

19 Felder, Duineveld, and van Assche, "Absence/Presence," 6; Degnen, "'Knowing,' Absence, and Presence."

20 Appadurai, *Future as Cultural Fact*, 3.

21 Carling and Collins, "Aspiration, Desire and the Drivers of Migration"; Nguyen, *The Displaced*.

22 Miceli, "The Capacity to Aspire of Children Immigrants"; Zetterstrom-Sharp, "Heritage as Future-Making."

However, here I refocus and extend the argument to displacement within Europe and with reference to the cultural heritage practices of refugees and forced migrants as displaced individuals.[23] The felt absence of intangible cultural heritage is a trigger that elicits personal future and cultural aspirations amongst displaced individuals. This happens through the reaffirmation, in the host country, of cultural traditions and heritage practices, which are thus both acknowledged and valued as resources fostering social and cultural cohesion and well-being. Such reaffirmation, however, can take place only through the individual and conscious reconsideration of "why" intangible cultural heritage matters and "how" it matters during displacement, so that it is possible to overcome the ordeal of forced movement and resettlement. Intangible cultural heritage and traditions matter to displaced groups and individuals; firstly because they are rationalized as mementoes and traces of their old selves, in the phase of displacement when sporadic glimpses of the past reemerge through the comforting memories of everyday gestures and meaningful rituals. Additionally, during the phase of the "absent presence," cultural traditions are perceived as goals and targets for a better future: by remembering and reintroducing them in their new everydayness, forced migrants and refugees have the hope to contest and alter their unfavourable conditions. As a consequence, cultural and heritage traditions become aspirational needs, personal wants, and individual and group expectations for a better future.

Therefore, I suggest that where these cultural traditions are rearticulated (because of an absent presence of heritage), this is done through narratives of resilience. While these narratives, in the longer term, could determine the creation of a shared heritage in Europe (or shared elements of such heritage), in the short and more immediate term, they can foster a sense of personal cultural worth and belonging. In the next section of this chapter, I consider resilient heritage as the result of narratives of hardship, identity, and remembering traditions.

Resilient Heritage: Narratives of Hardship, Identity, and Remembering Traditions

Between March 2016 and November 2017, I was in contact with a number of refugees and displaced individuals through charities (Rebuild Rethink Society, Manchester; Refugees Support Network, Manchester) and cultural associations (Syria Art Gallery, Nice), based both in the United Kingdom and France. Although it proved rather challenging to liaise with potential participants, I was able to carry out a set of twelve semi-structured interviews, aiming to understand whether displaced individuals would perceive the absence of heritage and to identify the meanings and purposes of heritage during displacement.[24] While I tried to reach out to the wider refugee community,

---

23 Ashworth, "Heritage and Local Development."
24 The project is ongoing, as it is my intention to expand the sample of interviewees to refugees and forced migrants from countries other than Syria. Overall twelve interviews (face to face, online, and via email, depending on the availability, location, and language skills of the interviewees) have

without favouring any ethnic group or nationality in particular, it is important to point out that most of the participants in this study were Syrian. This is because the Syrian refugee community is large and better known across Europe, and hence it is easier to approach.[25] The age of the interviewees ranged from twenty-one to fifty-eight years old, with ten of them being female and two male.[26] Through the interviews, two distinct and yet entangled themes (overcoming hardship through heritage, and remembering traditions) emerged. I explore these in the following section.

Overcoming Hardship through Heritage

All interviews started with a question addressing the ways in which participants would define their current status. This was mainly to understand whether, consciously or unconsciously, the "othering," the impersonal classification of "refugee" had been adopted by the individuals to justify their status and their (cultural) identity in the new country. The responses were polarized: on the one hand, participants gave a clear explanation of their professional identity and geographical origin (e.g., "I am a doctor originally from Syria"; "I am an artist from Syria and I came here four years ago"), and by doing so, they put an emphasis on their social role and cultural individuality. On the other hand, some of the interviewees simply replied by stating their displaced status (e.g., "I am a refugee"), hence subordinating any other cultural feature to the label of the "refugee" and to the loss of a personal, distinctive self. However, both types of responses shared heartfelt reflections on the hardship of their journey, on a physical and emotional level. The journey had catapulted them into a personal situation, cultural context, and social status where they did not want to be. This meant that all interviewees, although in different stages of their displacement, felt the need both to justify themselves for being refugees (the stereotyped "others") and to reiterate that they were in the hosting country not by their own will but because of external causes. As P4 said: "I am a refugee. Actually, I am a refugee only because I/we, are forced out of our own places; it is not optional for us to be here, it is not that we are here for leisure." Similarly, P9 voiced the feeling of having to justify their presence in the new context but also pointed out the importance of memories in the process of identity redefinition during displacement:[27]

---

been conducted so far. The interviewees were recruited via charities and cultural organizations, where one of the members of staff acted as the contact/liaison. Most of the refugees interviewed suffered from some mental problems, hence it was often necessary to carry out the interviews via email or with the support of a local translator. Their names were anonymized and coded as P (for Participant) followed by their interview sequence number (from 1 to 12).

25 Manchester is a "solidarity city," which means that it is part of the initiative on the management of the refugee crisis launched in the framework of the EUROCITIES network in 2012. Solidarity cities are committed to solidarity in the field of refugee reception and integration (https://solidaritycities.eu/about).

26 One of the interviewees was Afghani and one was Congolese.

27 Meyer, "Placing and Tracing Absence."

> [When you are a refugee,] you become a burden, someone that they have to place some-where: we used to be teachers [and] artists in our towns and now suddenly we have become no one. So you feel lost and you miss your family, friends, and things that you know, but then you remember your story, who you were before the journey, and you start to tell [it to] other people, and to share what you know, your religion, your costumes, your skills, so you show that you have a rich culture to offer.

All participants explained that feeling "unwanted" heightened their sense of longing for their cultural heritage, especially in the initial stage of their "resettlement," and a shared definition of heritage was identified: the interviewees defined heritage as "everyday rituals, religious ceremonies, and cultural traditions [which should be] celebrate[d] in the right ways" (P8). It was somehow present, although not visible, throughout their personal and physical journey: they carried it with them as traditional practices, which gave them a sense of pride and the strength necessary to overcome the difficulties they faced:

> [Heritage] reminds us where are we from. [...] I am now away from my country and from the war and I can be whatever I want to be, but the thing is, the way I grew up and how I used to live I believe is nice, so I am going to represent and protect what is right (P7).

When asked about the possibility of heritage being absent when people are displaced, participants unanimously clarified that an absence is felt only in relation to the inability to practise their traditions "as they should have been." This triggers a feeling of nostalgia for and an awareness of the richness of their cultural practices. Furthermore, through the interviews it emerged that cultural heritage practices are appreciated for their resilient quality: such traditions survive and "transcend wars and violence"[28] (P2) and are comforting resources through which they can fill the emotional voids caused by displacement. At the same time, cultural traditions are key elements for developing new meaningful connections in the host country, both with other refugee communities and with locals.[29] This confirms what Louise Ryan points out in terms of migrant groups and the ability to build, through cultural resources, new relationships that support them through their hardship.[30] Actually, by sharing, both with other displaced individuals and with local communities, their experiences and cultural traditions, forced migrants and refugees feel able to develop social and cultural bridges which not only foster a sense of belonging but also allow for a revaluation and appreciation of cultural practices like they used to be "when life was normal" (P1).[31] Hence, heritage traditions and practices may become a sort of intangible place to remember the trauma of displacement, but also to regenerate and nourish individual and cultural resilience.

---

28 Tangible heritage seems to be associated primarily with archaeological sites.
29 Simich, Beiser, and Mawani, "Social Support and Significant of Shared Experience."
30 Ryan, "Migrant's Social Networks and Weak Ties."
31 Halilovich, *Places of Pain.*

Remembering Traditions

Throughout the discussions, the interviewees revealed tragic and difficult personal stories. One topic of discussion revolved around the ways in which cultural traditions may have helped throughout the ordeals of journey and resettlement. Regarding this, most of the participants answered by saying that the "good memories" associated with their family ceremonies and rituals, and with the life left behind, gave them hope, strength, and willingness to persevere in the difficult moments. Through a selection of past, positive anecdotes associated with their cultural practices, interviewees explained that they found consolation, while in the new country/context, in remembering certain episodes or (sensory) elements of their way of living pre-migration—like the smell of the coffee that they used to drink with neighbours, family, and friends or the soothing nocturnal sounds of the cities before the war. Moreover, all of the interviewees pointed out that past episodes cannot be disentangled from their current condition, notwithstanding the dissonances: "my current story is composed of past and present," P12 explained, "so all parts of my story are important and it's like a chain. All the links are important and make up this chain and who I am now."

Marco Gemignani notes that refugees "look for solutions and comfort for their current [...] issues by remembering the 'cleaner water' of the pre-war times. Those memories extend beyond longing. They are sources of identity that tell them who they were and who they can be."[32] Indeed, all my interlocutors showed a strong connection between remembering cultural traditions, the need to communicate their identity while displaced, and a sense of belonging. P11, a Syrian PhD student based in Northampton, United Kingdom, used to be a well-known artist back in her hometown, and when asked about her memories in relation to heritage, she explained:

> I believe that the memories of my past and of traditions make us; we are built on our history. So memories make me the way I am like now, here: my personality, my history, how we grew up, how we learnt things, like respecting the older people, taking care of the neighbours, mercy for the younger, all those things.

Similarly, P6, a student from Afghanistan who arrived on his own in the United Kingdom when he was only sixteen years old, commented on how much the memories of his cultural traditions helped and motivated him during the journey from his country to the United Kingdom:

> We should remember our traditions; they are our way of living, [and] they make our identities even if, when we cross the borders, we have nothing. Even though they [the traditions] are in the past, they will motivate you. For example, when I travelled to come here, I was in a lorry. I did not know anybody, I had nothing with me, [and] I did not even have any more my phone, but during the travel, I thought of my traditions, I thought of the *nikha* and how beautiful it is and that I want to marry according to my tradition. I felt proud of my religion and my culture. This motivated me to continue, even if I was really

---

32 Gemignani, "The Past if Past," 146.

sad. One day, when the war ends, I will go back to my country and I will educate people there about our culture and traditions.[33]

The retelling of past events and the remembering of family ceremonies and the associated mundane sounds and smells are all part of a communicative memory of an unofficial heritage.[34] This unofficial heritage is concerned with cultural identities and sense of belonging, which refugees and forced migrants redefine every day and revalue throughout an iterative process.[35] However, these participants' responses show that "no memory is ever purely individual and always shaped by collective contexts":[36] it is inscribed into situated memories of past contexts, events, and people. These memories are always constructed and shaped by communal recognitions of (cultural) values, which constitute "who we really are" and which help to overcome hardship and the perceived absence of the selves.[37]

Concluding Thoughts

For displaced individuals, forced movements are not only about the physical and emotional journey, but also about the ways in which their cultural traditions can travel with them. Regarding this, Julia Creet has observed that "movement is what produces memory," which then changes the idea of the self, of others, of new and old places, and of the past.[38] During movements, a corpus of memories is, in fact, generated through the selective process of recollection. This process stems from the perceived absence (or what I call the "absent presence") of the familiar, an interruption of existing connections between people and their cultural heritage, which allows for an acknowledgment of missed traditions and the need to redefine them. The disruption of these connections means, first of all, that displaced individuals experience a loss of coherent relationships with what they used to know and what they used to practise as heritage before the imposed changes. Additionally, the feeling of disruption is exacerbated by the impossibility of carrying out such activities as they should be. This is not only because of the lack of people who understand and share the same values, materiality, and ultimately the same cultural heritage, but also because of the lack of a stable context which allows

---

33 The *nikha* is a religious Islamic marriage ceremony. This interviewee was Afghani.
34 Assman and Czaplicka, "Collective Memory and Cultural Identity"; Halbwachs, *On Collective Memory*.
35 Robertson, "Introduction: Heritage from Below."
36 Erll, "Cultural Memory Studies," 5.
37 Erll, *Memory in Culture*.
38 Creet speaks of a triple role of memory (identity forming, therapeutic, and community forming): for refugees, credible narrative memory is the key to refuge and migration. See Creet, "Introduction," 11–13.

individuals to feel safe and accepted and able to perform their heritage practices in their "true form."

However, this study has shown that displaced individuals tend to use the memories of cultural heritage, embodied into their everyday traditions, in an active and iterative way: cultural heritage traditions have been the means to overcome difficult moments and are useful to positively redefine their identities and culture in the hosting context. Through selected narratives of resilience about their traditional past practices, refugees, at least in the early phase of resettlement, move away from the absence of connections, from the endured suffering, and engage in an active and positive embrace of their past and cultural heritage. Their strength, now, as survivors, is in the positive memories and stories of what they used to do—as religious ceremonies, celebrations, mundane rituals—and of who they used to be—as legitimate individuals belonging to a rich culture.

Their heritage, as displaced individuals, is therefore a "resilient" one: it has the ability and capacity to recover quickly and frequently from the adversity of displacement. It is constantly reproduced, revalued, and readapted even in non-stable contexts and harsh circumstances by individuals and groups. It is a heritage that "draws on the ordinary and the quotidian, [and that] is underscored by embodied practices."[39] However, at the same time, it is a heritage "made in the shadows,"[40] away from the official and perhaps praising discourses of integration and multiculturalism. Resilient heritage is a key component of an acknowledged performative collective consciousness which links the past and the present in places where the distance with "home" is great. Furthermore, through the capacity to aspire, an almost primordial instinct that consents to find a balance between despair and utopia, resilient heritage nurtures a concrete awareness of cultural contributions to the host society and the possibility to recreate a feeling of belonging and pride in the self.

Through the acknowledgement of disrupted connections, this study has aimed to contribute to the understanding of an alternative framework of interpretation for intangible cultural heritage, conceived as cultural practices and traditions, within the context of displacement and displaced individuals. The study has focused on refugees based in Europe and their perception and definition of heritage during forced migration. It has identified a general, emerging discourse about the resilient nature of heritage, that is to say a heritage constantly produced, revalued, and adapted even in non-stable contexts and harsh circumstances. This has also stressed the importance of the awareness of the absent presence of heritage: a reflective phase within displacement that can help displaced individuals to identify values and memories and that can help them to give meaning to the present, as well as to reposition their cultural identities within the domains of cultural pride and of the capacity to aspire.

---

39 Robertson, "Introduction: Heritage from Below," 2.

40 Robertson, "Introduction: Heritage from Below," 7.

Bibliography

Appadurai, Arjun. *The Future as Cultural Fact: Essays on the Global Condition.* London: Verso, 2013.

Ashworth, Gregory J. "Heritage and Local Development: A Reluctant Relationship." In *Handbook on the Economics of Cultural Heritage.* Edited by Ilde Rizzo and Anna Mignola, 367–85. Cheltenham: Elgar, 2013.

Assman, Jan, and Jon Czaplicka. "Collective Memory and Cultural Identity." *New German Critique* 65 (1995): 125–33.

Carling, Jorgen, and Francis Collins. "Aspiration, Desire and Drivers of Migration." *Journal of Ethnic and Migration Studies* 44 (2018): 909–26.

Chatelard, Géraldine. *Survey Report: Intangible Cultural Heritage of Displaced Syrians.* Unesco, 2017.

Connerton, Paul. *How Societies Remember.* Cambridge: Cambridge University Press, 1989.

——. "Seven Types of Forgetting." *Memory Studies* 1 (2008): 59–71.

Creet, Julia. "Introduction: The Migration of Memory and Memory Studies." In *Memory and Migration: Multidisciplinary Approaches to Memory Studies.* Edited by Julia Creet and Andreas Kitzman, 3–28. Toronto: University of Toronto Press, 2011.

Degnen, Cathrine. "'Knowing,' Absence, and Presence: The Spatial and Temporal Depth of Relations." *Environment and Planning D: Society and Space* 31 (2013): 554–70.

Delanty, Gerard. "Entangled Memories: How to Study Europe's Cultural Heritage." *The European Legacy* 22 (2016): 129–45.

Erll, Astrid. "Cultural Memory Studies: An Introduction." In *Cultural Memory Studies: An International and Interdisciplinary Handbook.* Edited by Astrid Erll and Ansgar Nünning, 1–18. Berlin: De Gruyter, 2008.

——. *Memory in Culture.* Basingstoke: Palgrave Macmillan, 2011.

Felder, Martijn, Duineveld, Martijn, and van Assche, Kristof. "Absence/Presence and the Ontological Politics of Heritage: The Case of Barrack 57." *International Journal of Heritage Studies* 21 (2015): 460–75.

Frers, Lars. "Confronting Absence: Relation and Difference in the Affective Qualities of Heritage Sites." In *Heritage, Democracy and the Public.* Edited by Torgrim Sneve Guttormsen and Grete Swensen, 285–96. Farnham: Ashgate, 2017.

Gemignani, Marco. "The Past if Past: The Use of Memories and Self-Healing Narratives in Refugees from the Former Yugoslavia." *Journal of Refugee Studies* 24 (2011): 132–57.

Halbwachs, Maurice. *On Collective Memory.* Chicago: University of Chicago Press, 1992.

Halilovich, Hariz. *Places of Pain: Forced Displacement, Popular Memory and Trans-local Identities in Bosnian War-Torn Communities.* New York: Berghahn, 2013.

Harrison, Rodney. "Beyond 'Natural' and 'Cultural' Heritage: Toward an Ontological Politics of Heritage in the Age of the Anthropocene." *Heritage and Society* 8 (2015): 24–42.

——. "Forgetting to Remember, Remembering to Forget: Late Modern Heritage Practices, Sustainability and the 'Crisis' of Accumulation of the Past." *International Journal of Heritage Studies* 18 (2013): 579–95.

——. *Heritage: Critical Approaches.* New York: Routledge, 2013.

Harrison, Rodney, and D. Rose. "Intangible Heritage." In *Understanding Heritage and Memory.* Edited by Rodney Harrison, 238–76. Manchester: Manchester University Press, 2010.

Hetherington, Kevin. "Secondhandedness: Consumption, Disposal, and Absent Presence." *Environment and Planning D: Society and Space* 22 (2004): 157–73.

Hoelscher, Steven, and Derek H. Alderman. "Memory and Place: Geographies of a Critical Relationship." *Social and Cultural Geography* 5 (2004): 347–55.

Lacroix, Thomas, and Elena Fiddian-Qasmiyeh. "Refugee and Diaspora Memories: The Politics of Remembering and Forgetting." *Journal of International Studies* 34 (2013): 684–96.

Lucassen, Leo. "Peeling an Onion: The 'Refugee Crisis' from a Historical Perspective." *Ethnic and Racial Studies* 41 (2018): 383–410.

McDowell, Sara. "Heritage, Memory and Identity." In *The Ashgate Research Companion to Heritage and Identity*. Edited by Brian Graham and Peter Howard, 37–54. Aldershot: Ashgate, 2008.

McLean, Kate C., Monisha Pasupathi, and Jennifer L. Pals. "Selves Creating Stories Creating Selves: A Process Model of Self-Development." *Personality and Social Psychology Review* (2008): 263–78.

Meyer, Morgan. "Placing and Tracing Absence: A Material Culture of the Immaterial." *Journal of Material Culture* 17 (2012): 103–10.

Miceli, Simona. "The Capacity to Aspire of Children Immigrants." Unpublished conference paper.

Moran, Dominque, and Tom Disney. "'It's a Horrible, Horrible Feeling': Ghosting and the Layered Geographies of Absence–Presence in the Prison Visiting Room." *Social and Cultural Geography* (2017): 1–18.

Muzaini, Hamzah. "On the Matter of Forgetting and Memory Returns." *Transactions of the Institute of British Geographers* 40 (2012): 102–12.

Muzaini, Hamzah, and Claudio Minca. "Rethinking Heritage, but from Below." In *After Heritage: Critical Perspectives but from Below*. Edited by Hamza Muzaini and Claudio Minca, 3–21. Cheltenham: Elgar, 2018.

Naguib, Saphinaz-Amal. "Collecting Moments of Life: Museums and the Intangible Heritage of Migration." *Museum International* 65 1–4 (2013): 77–86.

Nguyen, Viet Thanh. *The Displaced: Refugee Writers on Refugee Lives*. New York: Abrams, 2018.

Robertson, Iain J. M. "Introduction: Heritage from Below." In *Heritage from Below*. Edited by Iain J. M. Robertson, 1–29. Farnham: Ashgate, 2012.

Ryan, Louise. "Migrants' Social Networks and Weak Ties: Accessing Resources and Constructing Relationships Post-migration." *Sociological Review* 59 (2011): 707–24.

Simich, Laura, Morton Beiser, and Farah N. Mawani. "Social Support and Significance of Shared Experience in Refugee Migration and Resettlement." *Western Journal of Nursing Research* 25 (2003): 872–91.

Smith, Laurajane. "The 'Doing' of Heritage: Heritage as Performance." In *Performing Heritage: Research, Practice and Innovation in Museum Theatre and Live Interpretation*, 69–81. Manchester: Manchester University Press, 2011.

——. "Intangible Heritage: A Challenge to the Authorised Heritage Discourse? Compilation." *Revista d'etnologia' de Catalunya* 40 (2015): 133–42.

——. *Uses of Heritage*. New York: Routledge, 2006.

Zetterstrom-Sharp, Johanna. "Heritage as Future-Making: Aspiration and Common Destiny in Sierra Leone." *International Journal of Heritage Studies* 21 (2015): 609–27.

Anna Catalani is Associate Professor at the Lincoln School of Design, University of Lincoln, United Kingdom. Anna's research has focused on issues of interpretation, identity construction, resilience, and memory across different cultural contexts and especially with regards to intangible cultural heritage and diasporas. Recently, in collaboration with Naresuan University, Thailand, Anna has been developing a body of research, funded by the British Academy, the Newton Fund, and the British Council, on heritage sites affected by flooding and local communities' responses to their preservation through intangible heritage practices (Lincoln School of Design, University of Lincoln, United Kingdom; email: acatalani@lincoln.ac.uk).

Acknoweldgements The author would like to thank all the participants in this research and the contributors to this volume, who generously shared their time, experience, and personal memories with me. She also would like to thank Dr. Amy Hetherington for proofreading this chapter and Dr. Kostas Arvanitis, Dr. Laia Colomer, and Dr. Sarah Feinstein for their constructive and valuable comments on the initial drafts of this chapter.

Abstract Migration facilitates collective and individual encounters, which contribute to the formation of a new heritage, in both tangible and intangible forms. However, amongst forced migrants and more specifically amongst refugees—the focus of this chapter—heritage needs to "die" first, before being recreated, redefined, and embedded into new shared cultural practices. This generates a rupture in memory and a perceived sense of absence with regards to heritage. Yet it is exactly this perceived sense of absence that can foster, within displaced people, the intention to revaluate and rearticulate their everyday cultural traditions. Using Appadurai's notion of the "capacity to aspire," this chapter discusses the idea of "resilient heritage," that is to say those forms of intangible heritage that survive trauma, which are reshaped through selective remembering and which nurture a sense of cultural worth and belonging especially in the earlier stages of resettlement.

Chapter 3

MUSEUM THEATRE, REFUGEE ARTISTS, CONTINGENT IDENTITIES, AND HERITAGE

ALISON JEFFERS

A MUSICIAN IN elaborate costume begins drumming an urgent rhythm as a large group of adults and children are ushered from the noisy foyer of Manchester Museum, leaving behind children's art workshops, the bustle of the café, and the gift shop. A storyteller in what looks like traditional Arab costume draws us upstairs saying, "Do you hear that? Do you hear that music, everyone? It means it's time. Come. We have to move, move quickly. The soldiers will be here any minute. Come with me if you want to be safe. Follow the music."[1] At the top of the stairs, we find ourselves in the Museum's Manchester Gallery dominated by the giant skeleton of Maharaja, an Asian elephant that lived in Manchester's Belle Vue Zoo for ten years in the late 1800s. Positioning himself beside the skeleton, the storyteller explains that the ruler's soldiers have

> chased us here, all the way to this United Kingdom, to England, to Manchester, to this Manchester Museum, because they want to stop the music. Because in my kingdom, this special music is forbidden. It's been hidden away for a thousand years. And forbidden, because it brings ancient magic back into the world. The ancient magic could bring hidden stories to life, the truth behind what we think we see. It conjures up the hidden world of the past—like this place does. In this museum the people from the past talk to all of us, through dresses and fabrics and earrings and weapons and combs and necklaces and fishing rods.

We are drawn into the next gallery by singing, ululation, and the rhythms of music performed by a live band fronted by an exuberant and engaging female singer. The storyteller explains that it's music from the Congo: "the music they would play every Saturday night, magic that would bring family and friends together." Performing in the entrance to the Living Cultures Gallery, the band is positioned in front of a huge glass case which displays wooden masks and carvings of human figures, some only six inches tall and some almost life size; the accompanying information informs the viewer that these were made in the nineteenth century by people in Kongo, Nigeria, and Ogoniland. On each side of the large central case stand eight dancers, wearing traditional Congolese clothing, gently moving to the music.

As the music fades, we are led into the Ancient Worlds Gallery. Here we encounter Ishtar, an ancient Babylonian goddess of love, beauty, and war who tells us that she has been robbed of her jewellery and belongings by museums and galleries in Europe. Pointing to a large stone slab on the wall, she recognizes it as part of her palace. "How did

---

I Martin et al., *Flying Carpets*. All quotations from the play are from this unpublished script.

it end up here? I don't remember giving it to you." She appears to read from the description beside the slab—"Europeans excavated sites all over the world and took the discoveries back to their own countries"—before turning to the audience and saying, "No wonder you have become rich." She tells us that she is being chased by bodyguards who want to take her back to the Louvre in Paris, having been warned by Mona Lisa that they will "capture me in a piece of frame and put me on display forever so they make money."

The character of Ishtar flees from the space, drawing us towards the Living Worlds Gallery, where we watch the final scene of a woman trying desperately to communicate with authorities in the United Kingdom about her council tax. In a moment of realization, she reveals that she always wanted to be a dancer, but "Dancing is a sin in my country. Dancing is a crime in my country. The only time I could dance was under the sound of lashes on my body. Dance from the depth of pain." Using words illuminated in neon around the gallery, she says, "In a few brief minutes, another person's life can become your own. Woman, dancer, child, mother, brother, the world, cities, countries, wildlife, migrant, refugee, stranger, human." Finally, turning to the audience, she says, "But imagine I could dance with you freely—so come now, come dance with me, let me take you to my galaxy," at which point she distributes small pieces of silver fabric among the audience and invites them to join her as the music of the sitar closes the scene and the performance ends on a celebratory note with music and dancing.

This chapter uses the example just described, a performance called *Flying Carpets*, "created and performed by refugee artists," to investigate questions of heritage, identity, migration, and performance.[2] *Flying Carpets* was part of Journeys Festival International (JFI), which aims to explore "refugee experiences through great art."[3] The artists in question were Firoozeh Fozouni, Serge Tebu, Emmanuela Yogolelo, Fereshteh Mozaffari, Mahboobeh Rajabi, Abas ElJanabi, and Arian Sadr, working with writer and director Cheryl Martin and Community Arts North West (CAN) in Manchester as creative producers. Yogolelo, Mozaffari, and Rajabi had been commissioned by CAN to each create a short performance piece as part of the "Manchester Museum Takeover" event, and these were woven into an overall narrative and promenade performance by playwright Cheryl Martin.[4]

---

2 ArtReach 2017. It is important that the terminology used to talk about this work, and the people who produce it, fairly and accurately describes the work and the artists without perpetuating inequalities and reinforcing power relationships. The phrase "refugee artist" is often used as a shorthand (and I have used it as such for this chapter), but many artists do not feel comfortable with it. In the *Flying Carpets* project, CAN attempted to avoid the term wherever possible, using "artists from refugee 'heritages'" instead. In more recent projects, CAN has used the expression "international artists," which they have found to be more positive, giving a greater sense of status and power to the artists involved (personal email to the author, Katherine Rogers, Exodus creative producer, CAN, August 29, 2018).

3 ArtReach 2017.

4 A promenade performance involves the audience moving to different locations to follow the action of the performance.

Based on observations of this piece in performance, access to the written script, sub-sequent visits to the performance site, and interviews with Mozaffari and Rajabi (two of the commissioned artists), I investigate some of the complexities of being a "refugee artist" in a heritage setting and the potential value that emerges of conceptualizing heritage and identity as contingent, used here to suggest the conditional, the accidental, the shifting. For refugees, this could imply a heritage that is "incidental" or "an indirect cultural byproduct, which is not intentional or cherished."[5] In the state of becoming "a refugee," an unwelcome personal, political, and social identity has been thrust upon unwilling citizens by war, hunger, torture, and violence or threat of violence. Legally, asylum seekers need to gain refugee status to stay in the "host country," and I have described this elsewhere as "bureaucratic performance," one of the paradoxes of refugee identity whereby asylum seekers "are forced to work hard to create an identity for which they have no desire but which they passionately desire at the same time."[6] In this chapter, I pursue this idea further by investigating the ways that refugee artists are mobilizing aspects of contingent identity in a heritage setting to challenge ideas of assuming a "refugee identity" at the same time as potentially destabilizing the identities of their audiences. I then use these ideas to reflect on current thinking and practice in museums and other heritage sites.

My proposition is that contingent identities can be utilized to the advantage of the migratory subject as well as for the benefit of the communities in which they find themselves. I carry out this argument by suggesting that theatre in museum settings has the capacity to highlight the *work* heritage does through embodying *articulations* of identity. Theatre and performance in museums not only considers theories of heritage and identity but build on them, amplifying and extending them through attention to practice. Contingent and processual aspects of heritage are illuminated by theatre and performance where heritage is seen as "a process [...] that reveals a multiplicity of narratives (or indeed sometimes conceals them)."[7] In the case of *Flying Carpets*, innovative theatre forms combine with radical museum practice to call attention not just to complex questions about identity and heritage among the refugee subjects, but also to demonstrate the capacity to challenge the assumed "stable" identities of the audience in challenging ways. In the following section, I set the stage by examining museum performance against a broad background of critical thinking about heritage and identity. I then discuss the idea of contingent identity using theories from theatre and cultural studies which emphasize questions of appearance and disappearance, visual instabilities and ghosts. Finally, I conclude by revisiting the example outlined earlier in this chapter to bring these sets of ideas together through thinking with Emma Waterton and Laurajane Smith about the importance of contingency in relation to the apparent stabilities of identity, heritage, and community.[8]

---

5 McCarthy, "Incidental Heritage," 60.

6 Jeffers, *Refugees, Theatre and Crisis*, 37.

7 Jackson and Kidd, *Performing Heritage*, 2.

8 Waterton and Smith, "Recognition and Misrecognition."

The "Work" of Critical Heritage Studies and the "Articulation" of Museum Performance

Recent critical studies emphasize heritage as a cultural product and a political resource "fundamental to constructs of identity."[9] Identity is understood here as a "multifaceted phenomenon that embraces a range of human attributes" which imply that "the sense of belonging to place [...] is fundamental to identity."[10] This is, of course, highly relevant when thinking about heritage in relation to refugees who are inherently displaced as much as to ideas about the communities that interact with museums more generally. Brian Graham, GJ Ashworth and JE Tunbridge recognize that in the late twentieth and early twenty-first centuries, "mass migration has created complex, multicultural societies" that have dramatically altered relationships between heritage and place, partly through generating a multiplicity of identities.[11] Citing Stuart Hall's ideas about the fragmentations of belonging that emerge from "the construction of diverse multicultural societies," Graham and his colleagues reiterate that identities "are never singular but [are] multiply constructed across different, often intersecting and antagonistic discourses, practices and positions."[12] Following this approach to heritage, the "normative and operational programmes" of organizations like UNESCO are eschewed in favour of "viewing heritage as the creative re-appropriation of the past, informed by the challenges of the present," stressing the need for generative rather than conservative approaches in heritage and museum work.[13] In a similar vein, Laurajane Smith discusses challenges to Authorized Heritage Discourse (AHD), which she claims is dominant in European policy and practice, concluding that there is "no such *thing* as heritage" because it is "a cultural performance [...] a process or a performance in which certain cultural and social meanings and values are identified, reaffirmed or rejected" rather than being "conflated with sites or places."[14] Smith's re-theorization of heritage as a performance places an emphasis on "the cultural 'work' that heritage does in any society."[15] I suggest in this chapter that the work of theorizing heritage can be tested out and articulated in the crucible of performance practice, and new ideas and discoveries fed back into both fields.

One way of articulating a political critique of community involvement in museums and other heritage sites has been through generating a more "interactive" experience, with theatre and performance in particular becoming a popular way to generate this interactivity. Critics concerned with the place of theatre and performance in heritage sites accept heritage as "a site of struggle [where] narratives can be contradictory, controversial and contested within and between cultures and communities."[16] Theatre

---

9 Graham, Ashworth, and Tunbridge, *Geography of Heritage*, 29.
10 Graham, Ashworth, and Tunbridge, *Geography of Heritage*, 40.
11 Graham, Ashworth, and Tunbridge, *Geography of Heritage*, 76.
12 Graham, Ashworth, and Tunbridge, *Geography of Heritage*, 81.
13 Alivizatou, "Intangible Heritage," 85.
14 Smith, "The 'Doing' of Heritage," 69.
15 Smith, "The 'Doing' of Heritage," 69.
16 Jackson and Kidd, *Performing Heritage*, 3.

scholars have paid particular attention to the ways that theatre can be used to create "energy exchange, interaction, [and] signification"[17] in heritage sites. Foremost in this field is the work of Anthony Jackson and Jenny Kidd, whose extensive study on performance and heritage is articulated in *Performing Heritage*.[18] Writing in this collection, performance scholar Baz Kershaw describes how theatre and performance in these sites "tends to dislocate normative epistemologies and ontologies, establishing creative environments" in which "contradiction and paradox" might set up "a radical dislocation of established knowledge."[19] Kershaw is keen to stress the sense of "disorder" that emerges in which memory is triggered in unpredictable and possibly contradictory ways and suggests that the "novel performance ecologies" generated by the encounter between theatre and heritage "reposition spectators unavoidably as participants rather than (or as well as) observers," thus destabilizing or revising their existing subject positions and epistemological certainties.[20] Jackson and Kidd discuss this as the "unsettlement of the audience"[21] in the moment of viewing theatre in museum settings. If we follow this line of thinking—that the experience of seeing theatre in a museum setting is inherently disordered, disruptive, and unsettling—then theatre performed in a museum setting by "refugee artists" serves to dislocate knowledge even further, possibly destabilizing what we think we know about ourselves as audience members, about refugees, and about the museum setting in which we are all located.

In the example of *Flying Carpets*, the creative strategies of mixing myth, history, and current reality created dramaturgical and scenographic effects that served to dislocate the site's knowledge and to prove the roles of the performers and audience members equally contingent. As I explain later in this chapter, the spatial dynamics of museum performance mean that the audience are often placed in a reflexive position, watching themselves watching the refugee performers, giving the performance what Kershaw describes as a "mirrors-within-mirrors quality."[22] I am interested in the idea that, as an audience, the value of not quite knowing, of being uncertain about exactly who or what we are looking at in refugee performance, especially in a museum space, can be a source of potential authority or influence for refugee artists and a useful corrective to a non-refugee audience whose assumptions and prejudices may thus be challenged. To understand this more clearly within the framework of Smith's "cultural performance," I now turn to scholarship in theatre, performance, and cultural studies because this will help to unlock some of the complexities of identity that emerge when theatre is created by refugee artists in a museum setting.

---

17 Kershaw, "Nostalgia for the Future of the Past," 135.

18 Jackson and Kidd, *Performing Heritage*.

19 Kershaw, "Nostalgia for the Future of the Past," 135.

20 Kershaw, "Nostalgia for the Future of the Past," 135.

21 Jackson and Kidd, *Performing Heritage*, 18.

22 Kershaw, "Nostalgia for the Future of the Past," 136.

Contingent Identities and the Value of Not Quite Knowing

Ghostly metaphors in connection to refugees are often invoked by campaign groups and by artists and writers. Church Action on Poverty, for example, set up the "Living Ghosts" initiative to draw attention to the links between refused asylum seekers and destitution. In their 2007 report, they suggest that "thousands of people refused asylum are living in the UK without any means of support—a ghost-like existence."[23] Theatre critic Lyn Gardner's review of *The Jungle* at the Young Vic in London called the refugee subjects of the piece "these living ghosts" in order to describe undocumented migrants living in the notorious Jungle camp in Calais.[24] Visual artist Arabella Dorman evoked similar feelings in her installation in St James Church, Piccadilly, London, in which she suspended 700 items of clothing abandoned by refugees on the Greek island of Lesbos. Commenting on the work, she said: "There were thousands of items of clothing discarded by refugees. I was struck by the concept of the empty garment, evoking the hidden presence of the person who had worn that item. These clothes reveal what is now being forgotten."[25] These ghostly metaphors suggest that campaigners and artists are drawn to the "liminal position between visibility and invisibility"[26] invoked by connections to ghosts. They suggest a strong sense of ambiguity—presence and absence, here and not here.

It may feel uncomfortable to use these ghostly metaphors in connection with refugees. However, metaphors around ghosts, spectrality, and haunting are arguably more responsible than those more commonly used to evoke overwhelming bodies of water such as waves, tides, or flows of migrants. Even arguably more benign metaphors around hosts and guests are still unhelpful, described as "old metaphorical habits that have naturalized the resemblance between the host and the national, the migrant and the guest."[27] Mireille Rosello notes the shift of perception implied when a new set of metaphors emerges from fiction (in this case the 2003 film *Dirty Pretty Things*) which helps us to consider relationships with refugees and migrants "according to a different grid" which "rewrites a familiar script without trying to erase it."[28] We need to pay attention to the "continuing liveness" of metaphors because it is never immediately obvious how they are being used, and this keeps them within a constant process of thinking through and negotiation.[29] In the context of thinking about refugees and performance in heritage sites, staying with metaphors and associations with ghosts particularly, and spectrality more generally, achieves three things: firstly, it draws attention to ideas about visibility in relation to refugees; secondly, it encourages attention to spatiality and spatial relationships; and thirdly, it focuses on questions of the contingency of identity connected to "refugee artists" and their audiences.

23 Church Action on Poverty, *Annual Review*.
24 Gardner, "The Jungle Review."
25 Sherwood, "Artist Hangs Refugees' Clothing in London Church."
26 Blanco and Peeren, *Spectralities Reader*, 2.
27 Rosello, "Wanted," 6.
28 Rosello, "Wanted," 17.
29 Peeren, *Spectral Metaphor*, 26.

Taking these points in order and thinking firstly about questions of visibility brings me to the work of theatre scholar Sophie Nield, for whom theatre is a valuable frame through which to talk about "identity, politics and experience"[30] by thinking about the complex ways in which visibility and invisibility work in performance and beyond. Describing the Victorian theatrical trickery of Pepper's Ghost, which was used to make people "disappear" on stage, Nield tells us that the trick lay in the fact that the disappeared person was still *present* on stage but that, through the use of mirrors, they were not *visible* to the audience. She uses this conceit to reveal the ways in which refugees can be made both visible and invisible, here and not here. In political discourse, for example, it is expedient *not* to see large numbers of refugees, perhaps when politicians are keen to stress the efficiency of border controls or the system for removing "refused" asylum seekers. In other circumstances, a large number of refugees planning to travel across the English Channel from Europe, for example, may be *conjured* to influence public opinion or gain resources for extra border protection. This is the negative side of contingency where refugees exist at the whim of public opinion, where a contingent identity is not helpful in gaining political agency or even in just surviving in a hostile place. However, I argue for the positive ways in which refugee artists can mobilize contingent identities, not only to express their own sense of identity but also to reflect back to audiences with apparently "stable" identities some sense of *their* own contingency as well; this brings us to the second advantage of paying attention to ghostly metaphors in relation to refugees and refugee artists in particular.

Spatiality and spatial relationships are emphasized in a theatrical setting which necessitates a focus on watching or viewing where "the space of the fiction, the space of the stage and the space of the audience" are "present and absent in different combinations."[31] For theatrical trickery such as Pepper's Ghost to be effective, the spaces of viewing and the spaces of performing must be controlled. The audience's sightlines must be managed by seating them in the fixed space of the auditorium, something which is possible in more traditional theatre settings but impossible to control in promenade performance, which moves around the museum building and where there is no strong demarcation of space. In the shifting spaces of a museum performance, where the position of audience and performer cannot be taken for granted, performers often speak with audiences in inherently ambiguous spaces where "the distinctions between performance space and audience space become [...] blurred and fluid [as a performer] converses with and often mingles with the audience."[32] The "energetics" of the performance—that is, "the interaction of living bodies and material site"[33]—are such that performers are often in close proximity to audience members.

I have already described the *Samedi Soir* scene in which the Congolese band beckoned the audience inside the Living Cultures gallery. The company had calculated that

30 Nield, "On the Border," 63.
31 Nield, "On the Border," 63.
32 Jackson, "Engaging the Audience," 13.
33 Kershaw, "Nostalgia for the Future," 133.

an audience of about thirty individuals would fit comfortably in the entry to the gallery in front of the band, and this had been the case for the first two performances of the takeover day. For the final performance, however, a group of about 100 people began to follow the storyteller and musician and the planned spatial relationships were hastily abandoned by both performers and museum ushers. Instead of standing to face the band and watch the performance from the front, the audience members were guided down both sides of a large glass case positioned in the middle of the gallery, so that they were effectively standing behind the band members, who were visible, but with their backs to us and obscured by the display case. Eight female performers maintained their positions down each side of the central glass case, dancing to the music only steps away from the audience members. This strange sense of dislocation and surprise was unplanned but provided one of the most effective moments in the performance when audience and performers occupied the same space. Any sense of demarcation was further blurred by the presence of the floor-to-ceiling glass case in the centre of the gallery through which we could see the rest of the audience and dancers on the other side, at the same time as having our own reflections mirrored back to us. The visual disorientation of this moment was heightened by the contents in the case, elaborately carved masks and strangely proportioned wooden figures, Japanese swords and armour, and, beyond that, rolls of cloth with intricate designs. The multiplicity of visual elements had the strangely destabilizing effect of immersing the audience into the action at the same time as distancing them from it by removing the intended visual stimuli of the band. We could imagine briefly that we were gathered at the *Samedi Soir*, swaying to the music and enjoying the atmosphere provided by the dancers, but we were simultaneously prevented from participation by gazing at the dancers and musicians through the mass of objects in the cases and thinking about their ambiguous relationship with both the space and the descendants of the people from whose culture they were taken. We were also looking at each other and perhaps wondering, like me, if other audience members were experiencing similar feelings of spectatorial uncertainty.

What were we really looking at? Thinking about the third value behind the visual instability associated with ghosts and spectrality brings me directly to thinking about contingent identity and refugee artists by "working *with* the metaphor."[34] Using spectrality to "call attention to and assign responsibility for social practices of marginalization and erasure, and for cultural and historical blind spots,"[35] means that seeing refugee artists perform in a heritage setting like a museum provokes questions about some of those "blind spots" and leads to speculation around issues of ownership, perspective, and belonging. If, as Hall suggests, "those who cannot see themselves reflected in the mirror [of the national heritage] cannot properly 'belong,'"[36] what exactly is happening when refugee artists stage the "takeover" of a major cultural institution and heritage site? If, indeed, the story of empire is "increasingly subject to a widespread selective

34 Peeren, *Spectral Metaphor*, 7.
35 Peeren, *Spectral Metaphor*, 13.
36 Hall, "Whose Heritage?," 220.

amnesia and disavowal" and is "largely narrated from the viewpoint of the colonisers,"[37] could it be that social memory which "foreshortens, silences, disavows, forgets and elides many episodes" has the potential to be seen from a different perspective as "the start of a different narrative"?[38] One of the exhibits in the Egyptian gallery is a modern-day life jacket, one of hundreds washed up on a beach which had been worn by refugees crossing the straits between Turkey and Lesvos. The life jacket exhibit was installed in 2017 along with a bag made from recycled life jackets. The objects are displayed to the public with the explanation that they are an example of "part of our new approach to collecting, to address current issues." Visitors can find out more about this particular exhibit and tweet their responses to a dedicated Twitter address at #MMlifejacket, and this might seem a practical and valuable way to start a different narrative around questions of migration and the role of museums in presenting present-day political and social challenges.

However, when I asked the artists whether they had been tempted to use this exhibit, Rajabi replied, "Honestly, no [...] for me through making work as an artist I realize now that the most powerful thing is to give you a different point of view. [...] I would like you to think differently."[39] The significant place Rajabi chose for her performance was not by the life jacket, but beside a glass case full of paper cranes, origami birds representing the 1,000 paper cranes started by Sadako Sasaki, a victim of the nuclear bomb dropped on Hiroshima in 1945, and said to have been completed by her friends when she died of radiation sickness. Rajabi recounted how she became fascinated by this story as a girl and had continued this interest into adulthood: "I was performing beside the Sadako cranes and I was saying to myself, 'This is a sign. I am performing beside a peace symbol in Manchester Museum after coming from Iran.' I've had all sorts of journeys in my life—so you can imagine that I became even more attached to this space."[40] The refugee life jacket would have told the sanctioned refugee story of vulnerability and crisis, the one the audience may have expected. As an artist, Rajabi was able to take inspiration from what interested and excited her more, intellectually and aesthetically, rather than respond to the expected object of the life jacket. Not only that, as an artist, she feels a responsibility to bring something new to the audience placing her in a position of power, an artist with something to offer rather than a suppliant refugee subject. Similarly, a different narrative allowed Mozaffari, an Iranian actor, to embody an ancient Babylonian princess who is angry "because she's come back and she can't find her people, her money [is] gone, her jewellery [is] gone, everything [is] gone,"[41] taken by the very institutional structures now hosting this story of dissent.

It is perhaps here that the ghostly metaphor begins to reveal its limitations and must give way to more concrete and political thinking about identity and agency. Where

---

37 Hall, "Whose Heritage?," 222.

38 Hall, "Whose Heritage?," 211.

39 Rajabi, interview with author.

40 Rajabi, interview with author.

41 Mozaffari, interview with author.

refugees are most closely connected to images of ghosts they are either in states of crisis or are undocumented and otherwise living outside normal legal and social limits. This is not the case for those refugee artists who are removed from such experiences of crisis, possibly only by time, but who seek to pursue an artistic career in their new home location: refugee artists struggling to reinvent themselves while still negotiating the difficulties of working through a new identity and the complications involved in leaving one set of heritages and living in another. Both artists I spoke to were taking the opportunity to develop their practice away from restrictions in their home countries, where "you don't have permission to express yourself, which includes freedom of speech, [which] includes art."[42] At the same time, they were also wary of being "put in the box labelled 'refugee artist.'" Rajabi talked about theatre being part of her identity, but she is also aware of being "fully international and of being passionate about Japan *and* being a "Manchester artist."[43] Mozaffari explained, "I want to be called an artist with a refugee background, or ethnic background, which is fine; it's part of my identity, I can't deny it."[44] The theatre piece allowed these women to emphasize their identity as artists, both using *and* playing down their refugee identity. At the same time, it enabled us as audience members to reflect on our own sense of contingency, perhaps destabilizing identities which are commonly perceived as, if not immutable, more "stable" than those of the refugee subjects performing. The final part of this chapter brings the conversation back into heritage discourse and thinking about the ways in which the *Flying Carpets* project might enable us to think through the too-broad conceptualizations of refugee, heritage, and community.

"Our Refugee Communities"

I employ Waterton and Smith's trenchant critique of the use of "community" in museum practice in order to reflect on the *Flying Carpets* performance and what it shows about the complexity of identity in heritage sites.[45] Arguing that the misunderstanding and oversimplification of community illustrates how "reified and unreflexive notions of community have been conveyed across the sector,"[46] Waterton and Smith argue that a "simplistic and romantic idea of community has been pedaled and pushed" onto all groups regardless of "class, racial or ethnic hierarchies."[47] As a result, "through the institutionalization of the trope of 'community,' a range of people suffer from status inequality and are thus unable to interact on terms of parity with heritage matters."[48] It is not uncommon to hear museum professionals using the phrase "our refugee communities" in informal

---

42 Rajabi, interview with author.

43 Rajabi, interview with author.

44 Mozaffari, interview with author.

45 Waterton and Smith, "Recognition and Misrecognition."

46 Waterton and Smith, "Recognition and Misrecognition," 5.

47 Waterton and Smith, "Recognition and Misrecognition," 7.

48 Waterton and Smith, "Recognition and Misrecognition," 10.

discussions around refugee arts. While we might be sympathetic to staff working in busy museums using a quick and easy shorthand, the flattening effect of thinking about "our community," whether that is refugees, museum professionals, or anyone else, is detrimental to innovative practices that seek to create relationships on a more meaningful and equitable level. It could lead to "heritage discourse and practices [that have] rendered communities, as much as their heritage, as subject to management and preservation"[49] rather than questioning and generation.

Thus, the exhibition of a life jacket in the Ancient Worlds Gallery opposite the Egyptian mummy is a gesture towards inclusion and a way to bring about an encounter between the ancient and the contemporary, but perhaps its real value in this instance is that it can also be ignored. Rajabi, as a "refugee artist," was not interested in telling the audience something they already knew, her choice instead being to select a site that interested her as an artist, to create a more poetic response to oppression, and to invite the audience to dance with her. For *Flying Carpets*, the element of choice offered to the artists created a sense of agency because the artists refused to be "othered" by the possible oversimplification of including a life jacket in the Ancient Worlds Gallery, for example. The *lack* of importance attached to this object is key in understanding some of the ways in which the reading of identity and community in the contemporary museum is multiply complex. In the performance of *Flying Carpets*, Mozaffari chose to confront the issues of appropriation and cultural acquisition head-on through assuming the character of the wronged goddess Ishtar. Rajabi chose to ignore the object most obviously attached to a "refugee narrative." We, the non-refugee audience, were confronted by a plethora of images and bodily sensations of proximity and distance in Yogolelo's *Samedi Soir* performance which served to destabilize our apparently stable identity.

A great many people are working very hard to move museum practice into a more dialogic relationship between the institution, the collections, and the public audience.[50] My goal in this chapter has been to both acknowledge and critique this work using the framework provided by critics in heritage, theatre, and cultural studies. I argue that performance in museum settings is one way to articulate, and possibly accelerate, understandings of the complexity of identity, heritage, and community. More specifically, theatre made in museum settings by refugee artists, where the artists are given agency and control over the settings and objects used, illustrates the ways in which their contingent identities can be mobilized to highlight the contingency of other apparently more stable identities, including the audiences who watch the performances and the institutions in which they are performed. Contemporary instabilities around identity and heritage are heightened by the numbers of people on

49 Waterton and Smith, "Recognition and Misrecognition," 11.

50 The appointment of Esme Ward (who had been Head of Learning and Engagement) as the first female director of the Manchester Museum in 2018 was seen as a move towards this kind of approach. www.museumsassociation.org/museums-journal/news/16022018-esme-ward-appointed-manchester-museum-director. Accessed June 13, 2018.

the move across the globe. Those engaged in heritage sites are increasingly involved in critical self-reflection about the history of their institutions and their ongoing relationships with the communities in which they are located. Theatre is often seen as a valuable and accessible way to "animate" heritage sites and to engage a wide variety of communities. I have tried in this chapter to reflect on these material realities at the same time as opening up some of the complexities that arise from placing theatre in these settings. Although performances are usually thought to be staged for the advantage of the audience, to educate or provoke them, they can also act as a positive experience for the (refugee) artists involved. On one level offering, of course, work and the opportunity for public creative expression, they can also be seen as a conduit for the exploration of personal identity as a refugee *and* as an artist. Furthermore, placing their performances in the unstable public space of the museum has the effect of unsettling the audience, who are perhaps led to reflect not just on the question of the refugee performer's identity, which ultimately remains closed to them, but also on their own sense of identity and belonging.

To respond to the broader questions raised in this volume, I suggest that thinking about refugee artists working in heritage sites can provide valuable insights into relationships between migration and cultural heritage. The creative platform museums and other heritage sites offer provides a rich background against which difficult questions of identity and belonging can be staged. The value of the instability of the museum space as a performance platform means that knowledge can be dislocated and apparently stable identities questioned for both performer and audience. The presence of refugees in the museum not as representatives of the "refugee community" but as independent artists with migratory backgrounds challenges not only authorized heritage discourse but also contemporary creative and political responses to it. However, while the museum can provide a site of sociocultural dialogue between migrants and local constituencies, conversations may prove difficult as much as, if not more than, productive; new gestures of openness, cultural awareness, ownership, and interactivity will erode historical inequalities only slowly. Listening carefully to artists with migratory backgrounds is one way to enhance and develop the conversation so long as these artists are permitted sufficient freedoms to explore not only the confluences but also the contradictions and even the hostilities that may underpin their relationship to heritage sites.

Bibliography

Alivizatou, Marilena. "Intangible Heritage and the Performance of Identity." In *Performing Heritage: Research, Practice and Innovation in Museum Theatre and Live Interpretation.* Edited by Anthony Jackson and Jenny Kidd, 82–93. Manchester: Manchester University Press, 2011.

ArtReach. *Journeys Festival International Programme.* Manchester, 2017.

Blanco, Maria del Pilar, and Esther Peeren, eds. *The Spectralities Reader: Ghosts and Haunting in Contemporary Cultural Theory.* New York: Bloomsbury, 2013.

Church Action on Poverty, *Annual Review*, 2007.

Gardner, Lyn. "The Jungle Review: Devastating yet Uplifting Story of the Migrant Crisis." *The Guardian*, December 17, 2017.

Graham, Brian, G. J. Ashworth, and J. E. Tunbridge. *A Geography of Heritage: Power, Culture and Economy*. London: Arnold, 2000.

Hall, Stuart. "Whose Heritage? Un-settling 'The Heritage,' Re-imagining the Post-nation." In *The Heritage Reader*. Edited by Graham Fairclough, Rodney Harrison, John H. Jameson Jr., and John Schofield, 219–28. London: Routledge, 2008.

Jackson, Anthony. "Engaging the Audience: Negotiating Performance in the Museum." In *Performing Heritage: Research, Practice and Innovation in Museum Theatre and Live Interpretation*. Edited by Anthony Jackson and Jenny Kidd, 11–25. Manchester: Manchester University Press, 2011.

Jackson, Anthony, and Jenny Kidd, eds. *Performing Heritage: Research, Practice and Innovation in Museum Theatre and Live Interpretation*. Manchester: Manchester University Press, 2011.

Jeffers, Alison. *Refugees, Theatre and Crisis: Performing Global Identities*. Basingstoke: Palgrave, 2012.

Kershaw, Baz. "Nostalgia for the Future of the Past: Technological Environments and the Ecologies of Heritage Performance." In *Performing Heritage: Research, Practice and Innovation in Museum Theatre and Live Interpretation*. Edited by Anthony Jackson and Jenny Kidd, 123–43. Manchester: Manchester University Press, 2011.

Martin, Cheryl, Fereshteh Mozaffari, Mahboobeh Rajabi, Serge Tebu, and Emmanuela Yogolelo. *Flying Carpets*. Unpublished manuscript, 2017.

McCarthy, Christine. "Incidental Heritage: Difficult Intangible Heritage as Collateral Damage." *International Journal of Heritage Studies* 23 (2017): 52–64.

Mozaffari, Fereshteh. Interview with the author. December 2017.

Nield, Sophie. "On the Border as Theatrical Space: Appearance, Dis-location and the Production of the Refugee." In *Contemporary Theatre in Europe*. Edited by Joe Kelleher and Nicholas Ridout, 61–72. Abingdon: Routledge, 2006.

——. "The Proteus Cabinet, or 'We Are Here but not Here.'" *Research in Drama Education: The Journal of Applied Theatre and Performance* 13 (2008): 137–45.

Peeren, Esther. *The Spectral Metaphor: Living Ghosts and the Agency of Invsibility*. Basingstoke: Palgrave, 2014.

Rajabi, Mahboobeh. Interview with the author. December 2017.

Rosello, Mireille. "'Wanted': Organs, Passports and the Integrity of the Transient's Body." *Paragraph* 32 (2009): 15–31.

Sherwood, Harriet. "Artist Hangs Refugees' Clothing in London Church to Highlight Crisis." *The Guardian*, December 13, 2017.

Smith, Laurajane. "The 'Doing' of Heritage: Heritage as Performance." In *Performing Heritage: Research, Practice and Innovation in Museum Theatre and Live Interpretation*. Edited by Anthony Jackson and Jenny Kidd, 69–81. Manchester: Manchester University Press, 2011.

Waterton, Emma, and Laurajane Smith. "The Recognition and Misrecognition of Community Heritage." *International Journal of Heritage Studies* 16 (2010): 4–15.

Alison Jeffers is Senior Lecturer in Applied Theatre and Contemporary Performance at the University of Manchester. She has written extensively on refugees and theatre, including *Refugees, Theatre and Crisis: Performing Global Identities*, published in 2012. Interested in questions of belonging, identity, citizenship, and socially engaged arts practices, Alison often works through practice and direct engagement with participants (Martin Harris Centre for Music and Drama, University of Manchester, United Kingdom; email: alison.jeffers@manchester.ac.uk).

Acknoweldgements I wish to thank Drs. David Calder, Lyndsey Garratt, and Aoileann Ní Mhurchú for their perceptive comments on an earlier draft of this chapter, and to the editors of this book for their helpful interventions.

Abstract This chapter examines the "takeover" of Manchester Museum as part of Journeys Festival International in 2017 to investigate some of the work that heritage does when refugee artists articulate questions of identity through performance in a heritage site. I investigate how a group of refugee theatre artists mobilized aspects of contingent identity, serving not only to explore their own identities as refugees and as artists but also to momentarily question the apparently stable identities of their audiences and of the heritage site in which they worked. The underpinning questions of this chapter concern holding open moments of surprise and uncertainty in the performance event and beyond: How can we acknowledge and accept levels of complexity and ambiguity engendered by creative work, while making artworks in heritage settings that explore delicate but urgent questions of justice, identity, and belonging? What can we learn about connections between migration and heritage when refugee artists "take over" a major cultural institution?

Chapter 4

MUSEUMS, ACTIVISM, AND THE "ETHICS OF CARE": TWO MUSEUM EXHIBITIONS ON THE REFUGEE "CRISIS" IN GREECE IN 2016

ALEXANDRA BOUNIA

Introduction

OVER THE PAST three decades, several cultural history museums in Europe and beyond have been trying to incorporate migrants and migration in their narratives, so as to include the history of migration in broader national stories.[1] The collections supporting these narratives usually consist of tangible and intangible evidence, objects such as travel and identity documents, certificates of birth, marriage, or education, photos, books, clothes, and personal or domestic items,[2] along with stories: memories from lands left behind, accounts of travel, and earlier trials. Pieces of luggage have been emblematic. Suitcases have become symbols of migration, of diaspora, of what it entails to leave home and go somewhere else, whether voluntarily or not.[3] The aim of such exhibitions is usually twofold: first, they encourage or facilitate integration and inclusion by recognizing, highlighting, and appreciating newcomers' contribution to their adopted land and society; second, they allow for the creation of new, more nuanced, and inclusive national histories.

Recent years have witnessed the publication of many works on migration and museums.[4] Some have been the result of research programs. Others represent the outcome of a long-standing interest in the museum world, specifically regarding how, as museums, we inclusively represent the "Other" within our institutions. Despite focusing

---

1 Naguib, "Collecting Moments of Life."

2 Lanz, "Staging Migration."

3 Poehls, "Europe, Blurred."

4 Bodo, Gibbs, and Sani, *Museums as Places*; Poehls, "Europe, Blurred"; Basso Peressut, Lanz, and Postiglione, *European Museums*; Chambers, De Angelis, Ianniciello, Orabona, and Quadraro, *Postcolonial Museum*; Cimoli, "Immigration"; Cimoli, "Identity, Complexity, Immigration"; Gouriévidis, *Museums and Migration*; Innocenti, *Migrating Heritage*; Whitehead, Eckersley, and Mason, *Placing Migration*; Whitehead, Lloyd, Eckersley, and Mason, *Museums, Migration and Identity*; Amal, Prenette, Lanouette, and Pâquet, *Musées, Histoire, Migrations*"; Lanz, "Staging Migration," 178–92; Levin, *Global Mobilities and Museums*; Bailey, *Interpreting Immigration*; Labadi, *Museums, Immigrants, and Social Justice*.

on exhibitions about the refugee "crisis,"[5] this chapter does not seek to add to the long list of publications. It aims to contribute to the discussion on museums as institutions that have social responsibility and that are activist institutions that cannot remain inert and numb to contemporary social issues. Of the many exhibitions organized in Athens and Thessaloniki in 2016, two are used to illustrate how museums are already trying to shed their sluggish, structured ways, to become agile, responsive, activist institutions, ready to collaborate with unconventional partners, like humanitarian nongovernmental organizations (NGOs). I argue that activism in museums needs to be put within a different framework to that which currently applies, suggesting instead that the "ethics of care" might provide a helpful theoretical framework for museums that would allow their activism to contribute to society in a real way. Therefore, this chapter is not about refugees and their inclusion in museums, but the author's reflections on how museums and heritage institutions might expand their role by supporting and engaging people in need, to become a platform for heritage discourse that is more attuned to the demands of contemporary societies.

A Brief Background

From March 2015 to March 2016, when the EU–Turkey agreement was signed, almost a million migrants and refugees (mainly from Syria, Afghanistan, Iraq, Iran, Pakistan, and Somalia) arrived in Europe by crossing the Aegean Sea, risking their lives in an effort to escape war, violence, and poverty.[6] Many died in the journey; others saw loved ones perish at sea. The human tragedies were recorded and disseminated across European media. Global and national humanitarian organizations and volunteers rushed to the Greek islands to offer help. For the first time, international organizations, such as the Office of the United Nations High Commissioner for Refugees (UNHCR), created stations on European soil. The flow of people arriving on the Greek islands was directed first to Athens, and then to the north of the country, to Idomeni, where they usually stayed for a few days before starting their journey via the "Balkan route" towards Northern Europe. In March 2016, the northern borders of Greece were closed to refugees and the journey onwards became almost impossible. To this day, nearly 65,000 refugees remain in Greece in often "unbearable" conditions.[7] The situation has created strain and discontent amongst local communities, which has in turn generated negative responses on the local level, often supported by nationalist groups.

In this time, the role of NGOs became increasingly important. In September 2015, minor civil society actors who had been first responders to the influx of refugees in

---

5 This is the term used, in a rather Eurocentric way, to describe the increased movement of refugees mainly from Syria, but also from other countries, such as Afghanistan and Iraq, to Europe via the Greek islands and Italy over the summer of 2015 and the first few months of 2016.
6 "Regional Refugee and Migrant Response Plan for Europe. Eastern Mediterranean and Western Balkans Route, January to December (update May 2016)," UNHCR, 2016 PDF, 45.
7 "Greece Factsheet, September 2018" (Greek version), UNHCR, 2018; Stubley, "Greece's Moria Refugee Camp"; Nye and Sands, "UN Urges Greece to Act."

Greece started being gradually replaced—at times in a tense manner—by larger and more professional organizations, such as UNHCR.[8] In February 2016, legislation was enacted limiting the role of volunteers and minor civil society actors (Law 4368/2016), and the hegemony of professional NGOs came to be the norm. Some considered this a much needed professionalization of relief operations and a sign of action and control on behalf of the authorities; others saw it as yet another form of top-down state control and exercise of hegemonic power.[9] In any case, the role of NGOs remains a source of controversy and debate.

Museums, Migration, Refugees, and the "Ethics of Care"

Museum initiatives that address or respond to humanitarian phenomena like the refugee crisis usually start following the traumatic event, when the people involved have reached their final destination and are in a position to start reflecting on their experiences. These initiatives usually overlook the complexity of the phenomena, which involve different actors: the people on the move, local receiving communities, humanitarian workers, civil society actors, and local and governmental authorities. The politics involved in these cases are often complicated. How can museums discuss, for example, the ambivalence of the state or other funding authorities in approaching social crises? How can museums respond to an *ongoing* phenomenon filled with traumatic personal situations? Should museums be involved in this process as it unfolds, or should they wait until it is finished (has become history) so that it is a safer topic to discuss? Is documenting people's experiences and memories as refugees as important as helping them? More important, how can museums go beyond their position as "social mirrors"[10] reflecting past events, to become active participants in what is currently happening, that is, as "social commentators" but also "shapers."[11]

Museum professionals have started arguing that museums should take stronger positions: to use the power and trust they enjoy to take explicitly political stances, and to become "activist museums."[12] An activist museum is an institution that does not just narrate, but also *creates* cultural realities, considering it a duty to expose and combat injustice. An activist museum goes beyond its usual participatory and inclusive practices, that is, representing the underrepresented and collaborating with communities. Schellenbacher[13] argues that activist museums need to consider four principles: an explicit agenda, reflection of activism across all aspects of their work, concrete offerings of action for their visitors, and space for opposing opinions, however controversial these might be.

---

8 Skleparis and Armakolas, "Refugee Crisis."

9 For a description of the variety of actors involved during the crisis, see Papataxiarchis, "'Being There.' Part I"; Papataxiarchis, "'Being There.' Part II."

10 Rhys and Baveystock, *Collecting the Contemporary*, 15.

11 Cf. McFadzean, "Museums"; Rhys and Baveystock, *Collecting the Contemporary*, 15.

12 Message, *Museums and Social Activism*.

13 Schellenbacher, "Empowering Change."

In the case of refugees, international cultural associations and professionals are encouraging museums to become activist and take an explicitly pro-refugee stance. More specifically, these actors are suggesting that museums act by: "Raising awareness within receiving communities and triggering responses; [...] Enhancing conditions for refugees by providing venues for activities; [...] Facilitating interaction and thus enhancing integration; [...] Becoming coordination hubs and collaborating with NGOs, government and non-government authorities to provide immediate support."[14] In other words, museums are being urged to become spaces where relations can be built, support can be gathered, integration can be facilitated, and community cohesion and awareness can be raised.

I argue that this support also encourages museums to go beyond activism, to reflect harder on their role and place within society, and to reconfigure them by taking a clear social perspective in line with the political and philosophical theory of the "ethics of care," which is rooted in feminist political theory. The ethics of care is also connected to the concepts of trust, mutual consideration, and solidarity, as well as civil society and human rights.[15] Care, unlike interest, duty, or obligation, is an ethical practice and attitude that requires a reaching out towards something beyond the self.[16] "To care" means to recognize histories of injustice, not only via empathy, but also by taking responsibility for injustice, as well as for the system that produces it and allows people to be treated differently. It therefore goes beyond "taking a stance," and works on the whys and hows of injustice and anything that supports it.[17] The ethics of care has been developed as an alternative theory to dominant moral approaches. It focuses on "attentiveness, trust, responsiveness to need, and narrative nuance"; it is an approach that "fosters social bonds and cooperation."[18] It gives centre stage to the community and not the individual, and values emotions such as empathy and shared concern, while allowing for a reconsideration of the social and political institutions (such as museums) in society.[19]

Tronto[20] identifies four phases of care: first, "caring about" someone or something means that individuals and societies recognize needs in others and offer them their attention and support. The object of care is important, as it defines the caring entity. Second, "taking care of" someone or something means realizing that something can be done and acting on this realization. It elevates the notion of responsibility to a moral category, and prioritizes it over those of "obligation" or "compassion." Third, "care-giving" means to be practically involved in offering care and satisfying human need, and thus acquiring competence and confidence in caring. Fourth, "care-receiving" means making sure that the care work has been done, acknowledging the difference in perceptions of

---

14 NEMO, *Museums, Migration and Cultural Diversity*.

15 Held, *Ethics of Care*; Koggel and Orme, "Care Ethics."

16 Tronto, *Moral Boundaries*; Till, "Wounded Cities."

17 Till, Kaufman, and Woodward, "Place, Memory, and Archive."

18 Held, *Ethics of Care*, 15.

19 See Held, *Ethics of Care*, 130; Tronto, "Care as a Political Concept," 145; Tronto, "Creating Caring Institutions."

20 Tronto, *Moral Boundaries*, 105.

care, and allowing for responsiveness, which often means recognition of difference and listening to others, as well as creating space for different views and ideas.[21] These four phases of care can be used to review and reflect on individual and institutional practices and, therefore, encourage an alternative way of looking at both social structure and power.

The ethics of care provides an interesting lens through which to analyze and understand the work undertaken by museums in Greece, but also to reflect on how museums could move towards redefining their role in society. I now present two exhibitions that took place in 2016 in Athens and Thessaloniki. These exhibitions alone do not necessarily qualify the respective institutions as "activist museums," as they did not affect all aspects of museum work or initiate a radical change in the museums' approach to contemporary issues.[22] That said, I argue that they did encourage the development of the ethics of care, which ultimately helped trigger a new understanding of the institutions' role and relationship to society. This was done, first, by raising awareness of the need to "care about" refugees, by highlighting the fact that receiving communities had already "taken care of" those in need and encouraging the former to continue "giving care," as in the case of the campaign exhibition by Amnesty International and Oxfam; and, second, by raising awareness of the fact that "giving and receiving care" is everyone's responsibility, as in the case of the exhibition of the Museum of Photography. These events continue to provide opportunities for museums and museum professionals to reflect and reconfigure their role in society and their responsibility to act.

The refugee crisis of 2015–2016 caught Greek museums unprepared. With the exception of the Archaeological Museum of Thessaloniki—which had planned an exhibition of antiquities brought to Greece in 1922 by Greek refugees leaving Rhaidestos[23] and was therefore in a position to contextualize the exhibition with reference to current events—no institution could present an exhibition reexamining the stories of its collections or presenting them in a new light, as advised by the Network of European Museum Organisations (NEMO).[24] Nevertheless, in 2016, a number of temporary exhibitions opened across a number of Greek cities (e.g., Athens, Thessaloniki, Mytilene, Ioannina), primarily addressing two genres: first, artistic installations, often incorporating iconic objects, such as the rafts or orange life vests; and, second, photographic exhibitions, using photographs by photojournalists closely following the crisis events in real life, as well as images by less well-known photographers, artists, or even amateurs.

The exhibitions discussed in this chapter belong to the second genre. They were both organized and presented in the period from May to December 2016, which came soon after the agreement reached between Turkey and the European Union (March 2016), encompassing a time in which the refugee issue was high up on Greece's political and social agenda. Both exhibitions were based on an unconventional practice, specifically, collaboration between museums and NGOs—especially in a time when the role of

---

21 Tronto, *Moral Boundaries*, 108; Till, "Wounded Cities," 11.

22 Cf. Schellenbacher, "Empowering Change."

23 Veleni, Tsangaraki, and Chatzinikolaou, *Rhaidestos–Thessaloniki*.

24 NEMO, *Museums, Migration and Cultural Diversity*.

NGOs was relatively controversial. Their aim and approach was explicitly activist, while encouraging different levels of the ethics of care.

The Campaign-Exhibition: "A Museum without a Home"

"A Museum without a Home—An Exhibition of Hospitality" was a campaign-exhibition organized by the Greek section of Amnesty International and Oxfam (November 11 to December 12, 2016). It consisted of a series of large-scale posters, each depicting real, yet ordinary, often mundane items (such as colouring crayons, a cup and a saucer, toys, a jacket, a shirt, or a drum) that Greeks had donated to refugees as an act of solidarity and friendship. The posters were displayed at bus and tram stops, inside metro stations, and on trains around Athens, "transforms[ing] the city into a 'museum,' acknowledging, showcasing, and celebrating the solidarity of the Greek people towards people fleeing their country and calling on Greeks and people—as well as leaders—worldwide to pledge to support dignity and safety for all."[25] At the same time, real objects were displayed in museums around Athens: the Acropolis Museum, the National Museum of Contemporary Art, the Frissiras Art Museum, the Museum of School Life and Education, and the Stavros Niarchos Foundation Cultural Center. The posters also carried explanations regarding the donors and recipients of the items displayed on the posters. Short videos were made available on YouTube, providing testimonies and offering very personal insights into the process of giving and taking.[26] The exhibition and supporting resources encouraged viewers/visitors to contribute to the efforts of Amnesty International and Oxfam, whereas the exhibition's website encouraged visitors to sign a pledge.[27] The exhibition went on tour in 2017 to Ioannina, Serbia (Mikser Festival—Migration 2017), and New York (72nd United Nations General Assembly), and even received a European Excellence Award in 2017 under the category "NGOs and Associations." In June 2018, the exhibition was presented in Glasgow.[28]

The exhibition was fully organized by the two NGOs, with the museums lending their names to the effort, thus supporting the campaign on a symbolic level. The word "museum" in the campaign-exhibition's title, as well as the long list of supporting institutions, bolstered the gravitas of the initiative. The exhibition had all the characteristics of a "pop-up," that is, a temporary installation of an experimental and ephemeral nature that aims to facilitate discussion around an important but difficult topic.[29] Something between an exhibition and a form of experiential marketing,[30] this project aimed to communicate a

---

25 Press release, original in English, n.d. It was available online: https://oxfam.org/en/refugee-and-migrant-crisis/museum-without-home-exhibition-hospitality-goes-live-exhibits-all-around. Accessed September 30, 2018.

26 For a series of testimonies regarding the exhibits, see www.youtube.com/channel/UCbP2O-2UJx61W_RpbU0wJzg. Accessed February 2, 2019.

27 The website www.museumwithoutahome.gr/en is no longer available.

28 See www.youtube.com/watch?v=O6YktvYMf2I&t=5s. Accessed February 2, 2019.

29 Grant, "Pop-Up Museums."

30 Walhimer, "Pop Up Museum."

Figure 4.1. "A Museum without a Home" exhibition poster as displayed on one of the metro trains in Athens. (Author image: Alexandra Bounia)

strong message about refugees to an audience not necessarily engaged with museum institutions—a message of commonality and immediacy, arguing that we are all people sharing the same needs, and that offering solidarity and support does not require a lot of effort. The initiative sought not only to raise awareness of events but also to inspire people to do something on an individual level, such as donating or volunteering. In other words, it sought to increase awareness about the need to "care for," and to involve people in "care-giving." In addition, by showing the acts of solidarity that had already taken place in Greece, this pop-up event aimed to create a positive feeling among the Greek audience to whom the exhibition was initially addressed, to offer praise for the support offered by the Greek people during the crisis, and to show that they had, in fact, already made efforts to "take care of" refugees. The museum partnership gave credibility to the exhibition, and provided a connection between the material world—the objects—and the ideas of giving and sharing, making this initiative more than just an advertising campaign.

From the perspective of the museums, experimenting with pop-ups and campaigns is an attempt to think differently about who they are and what they can do. The practice was not without its challenges, first because the institutions were essentially campaigning for NGOs, second, because in doing so, they effectively questioned the primacy of their collections in exploring social issues, and finally because they were addressing a diverse audience. This pop-up museum alliance further offered the opportunity to bridge institutional and personal views, to memorialize small, everyday acts of kindness, and to thus "monumentalize," celebrate, and elevate them to acts that deserve to be remembered. In other words, the use of the term "museum" to describe this campaign, but also the collaboration with institutions of various sizes, impact, and prominence, aimed to emphasize the exhibition's message about the importance of contributing and supporting. The project press release noted:

> The "Museum without a Home" is a tribute to the history that is being made by contemporary Greek citizens, who supported in a very difficult period of time people who had to leave their country in search of safety and dignity. It is a "museum" dedicated to humanity and hope, two values that we cannot allow to fade.[31]

The tone is emotional and strives to connect with history. Moreover, it highlights the historical importance of what is currently happening in the country to elicit as much support as possible. It offers the reassurance that the nation has done its best. Small acts of kindness are immortalized and the feelings of citizens of Athens or other Greek cities—i.e., exhaustion after such a long period of turmoil, difficulties, and changes—are construed as natural and human, the result of a "good fight" which was both successful and deserving of celebration. The personal testimonies of those who had donated the items and the recipients were also meant to indirectly encourage further solidarity, support, and hospitality, by emphasizing the fourth dimension of the ethics of care—i.e., "care-receiving."[32]

---

31 Press release.
32 Poehls, "Europe, Blurred," 337–53.

Awareness and Compassion Are Not Enough: Taking Responsibility through "Another Life"

The exhibition "Another Life: Human Flows, Unknown Odysseys" was inaugurated at the Thessaloniki Museum of Photography[33] in May 2016 (from May 31 to November 15, 2016). More than 160 photographs by twenty-six photojournalists were on display. Some photographers were well known and celebrated,[34] while others were younger and less well known, but equally active in recording the refugee crisis as it unfolded in Greece. The exhibition was divided into two sections: the first focused on the arrival of refugees on the Greek islands, and the second presented the start of their journey from northern Greece towards Europe, through what is known as the Balkan route. In addition, to show how long the phenomenon had been occurring in Greece, the exhibition included photographs taken before 2015. Photographs were also projected depicting the relationships of refugees with local society, groups, and collectivities dating from the visit of Pope Francis to Lesvos in April 2016 to the evacuation of the Idomeni camp in May 2016.

The curators' text accompanying the press release for this exhibition focused on stirring emotion and empathy. The curators used emotive words such as "uprooting," "deep pain," "victims of a cruel war," "poverty [...] transmitted almost like a disease," "broken people," "despair of those who sleep exposed on a strange land," "[people] trapped across fences of all sorts," and "[people] that roll on the side of the road as unresolved suspense" to imbue the exhibition with a particular feeling.[35] The same text explained the rationale behind the chosen photographs: while they could be critiqued for displaying reality in a brutal form, they also highlighted the pain and distress experienced by refugees, therefore revealing the unequal power relations at play and giving voice to the underrepresented. The museum responded to criticism on the effectiveness of the medium used,[36] arguing that theoretical concerns about the use of photography do not diminish the power of the medium to give voice to those in need of help. In fact, the aim of the exhibition was to give such a voice. Other than professional photojournalism, the exhibition also included amateur photographs (selfies, snapshots, and screenshots) by two young Syrian refugees, while on a second projection, images from social media (what is known as "citizen journalism") were displayed, highlighting the solidarity shown by groups and individuals towards refugees. This is particularly relevant especially as the exhibition took place in the Museum of Photography, which is housed in an old warehouse in the port of Thessaloniki and was at the time sharing its location with a refugee camp. As the curator, Penelope Petsini, observed: "It is very difficult, very complicated to present something that is unfolding right now, while showing respect for the people who might come into the exhibition and see their lives on the wall; not a history that happened

---

33 www.thmphoto.gr.

34 For example, Alkis Konstantinidis, Aris Messinis, and Yannis Behrakis. A full list of participating photographers is available in the exhibition catalogue.

35 This text was disseminated together with the press release, and was also available on pages 12 to 13 of the exhibition catalogue (Thessaloniki: Thessaloniki Museum of Photography, 2016).

36 Cf. Stylianou and Stylianou-Lambert, *Museums and Photography*, 6.

elsewhere, to somebody else."[37] The statement clearly reflects the ethical concerns around the exhibition's curating practices and goals, which were further clarified:

> A critical informed representation of the world can still maintain humanist values in common view, can contribute to stand by the weak, can artistically build an image which allows both *emotional identification* and *moral commitment for action*, without concealing the workings of the media world or uncritically consecrating photography.[38]

The museum uses the exhibition to highlight the public's ethical responsibility, "*not just for solidarity reasons*, but so that we know that the social issues, issues of social justice, do not have borders; they *create obligations* and ask each of us to take a stance, today" (emphasis added).[39] It is therefore not just a matter of taking a stance, but an issue of ethical responsibility that goes beyond obligation. Accordingly, this exhibition in particular is not just about raising awareness. It is about creating commitment, encouraging action, making a political statement, and urging visitors to be not only aware but also involved. The political activism was also complemented at the time with a practical call for action. In fact, for the duration of the exhibition, the municipality of Thessaloniki collected supplies for distribution amongst refugees, whereas a list of required items could be found on the museum website.

Conclusions

The 2015–2016 refugee crisis presented an opportunity and a challenge for Greek museums. It provided a real and urgent opportunity to rethink their role in society and to act, to overcome their reluctance to be involved in the contemporary context, and to respond in a socially responsible way. The social role of museums is multifaceted: curating human relationships, providing opportunities for discussion on diversity and reflection on social change, inviting audiences to present their views, to debate them, and to reach the point where they value and respect different ideas and approaches, providing spaces for sharing experiences and knowledge, and serving as spaces for human compassion and humanity. The exhibitions discussed aimed to do all of these. They had the common aim to raise awareness, to make people reflect on refugee issues, and to invite them to discussions and debates; to cultivate humanism but also to make a political point; to curate views and not just collections; to take a stance and to invite others to share it. Both exhibitions had clear intentions: to inform, shock, and shame, but also to comfort and praise. Their purpose was to make people feel, empathize, remember, and, eventually, respond by donating items, money, and time, or by signing a pledge.

However, the exhibitions first and foremost aimed at developing relationships of care: to foster and celebrate social responsibility, sentiments of solidarity, even affection and attachment. They aimed to go beyond the cultivation of respect and feelings of justice, to support the development of a deeply affective and caring relation between persons,

---

37 Interview given to TV100, www.youtube.com/watch?v=uKHD0i9G5fY. Accessed October 12, 2018.

38 Original in English, Papaioannou and Petsini, "A World of Agony," 138, emphasis added.

39 Andreas Takis, interviewed by TV100, www.youtube.com/watch?v=uKHD0i9G5fY. Accessed October 12, 2018.

regardless of their current status. They aimed to make people engage in common projects, to highlight similarities and a form of responsibility that had not previously existed.[40] In this sense, the exhibitions, albeit in different ways, aspired to stimulate the ethics of care in their audiences. The exhibitions acted as processes—their temporary nature reinforcing the process element—through which an ethical perspective towards the refugee crisis was built, one that relied on forming relationships between refugees and the receiving societies, based on their shared humanity. Views on social relationships were transformed by assigning responsibilities of care to visitors or pointing out that they were well placed to provide care, and that they had, in fact, already participated in such assignments. The exhibitions also intended to connect the personal and the political and to introduce a "care thinking" in the political decisions made on an individual as well as on a social level.

These exhibitions, albeit political, in the sense that they emphasized the care given or received as an ethical, political, and ideological position, also encouraged and cultivated the development of a different social structure. The museum, therefore, is not just a place of representation, inclusion, or exclusion. It is not just a place where affect is created or put into action to develop compassion and understanding. It is not just a venue for activities, interaction, or integration. It becomes a place where a clear moral stance is adopted and cultivated. The ethics of care means taking not only action but also responsibility for action, as well as responsibility for inertia. In this sense, the museum is realized as deeply political, and not only an activist institution. It aims to restructure society through a discourse of care, by making it realize its own power, as well as the importance, interrelations, and complexities of acting and caring. Far from offering abstract moral suggestions, museums need to be practically involved in "care-giving," while creating a space for "care-receiving."

These exhibitions are examples of how museums and heritage institutions can respond to cultural, social, and political changes as they happen in the world. New partnerships can be developed and cultivated that would allow museums to learn from the practices of others, like civil societies and NGOs, and to experiment with different ways of advocacy. Museums can adapt their practices and discourses to be able not only to respond in a faster and more efficient way to societal needs but also to reconfigure their role in society, to critically reflect, encourage novel partnerships, and undertake daring initiatives. This might go beyond signifying a new role for museums and heritage sites, to also extend to a new cultural, social, and political reality around the world.

Bibliography

Amal, Marianne, Yves Prenette, Mélanie Lanouette, and Martin Pâquet, eds. *Musées, Histoire, Migrations*. Québec: Presses de l'Université Laval, 2015.
Bailey, Dina A., ed. *Interpreting Immigration at Museums and Historic Sites*. Lanham: Rowman & Littlefield, 2018.

---

40 Cf. Held, *Ethics of Care*, 131.

Basso Peressut, Luca, Francesca Lanz, and Gennaro Postiglione, eds. *European Museums in the 21st Century: Setting the Framework*. Milan: Politecnico di Milano, 2013. https://issuu.com/melaproject/docs/melabook_07_vol2_hq-single_page. Accessed January 27, 2020.

Bodo, Simona, Kerstin Gibbs, and Margherita Sani, eds. *Museums as Places for Intercultural Dialogue: Selected Practices from Europe*. MAP for ID, 2009. www.ne-mo.org/fileadmin/Dateien/public/service/Handbook_MAPforID_EN.pdf. Accessed January 27, 2020.

Chambers, Iain, Alessandra De Angelis, Celeste Ianniciello, Mariangela Orabona, and Michaela Quadraro, eds. *The Postcolonial Museum: The Arts of Memory and the Pressures of History*. Farnham: Ashgate, 2014.

Cimoli, Anna Chiara. "Identity, Complexity, Immigration: Staging the Present in Italian Migration Museums." In *Museums, Migration and Identity in Europe*. Edited by Christopher Whitehead, Katherine Lloyd, Susannah Eckersley, and Rhiannon Mason, 285–316. London: Routledge, 2015.

——. "Immigration: Politics, Rhetoric and Participatory Practices in Italian Museums." In *Museums and Migration: History, Memory and Politics*. Edited by Laurence Gouriévidis, 83–102. London: Routledge, 2014.

Gouriévidis, Laurence, ed. *Museums and Migration: History, Memory and Politics*. London: Routledge, 2014.

Grant, Nora. "Pop-Up Museums: Participant-Created Ephemeral Exhibitions." *Exhibitionist* Spring (2015): 14–18.

Held, Virginia. *The Ethics of Care: Personal, Political, and Global*. Oxford: Oxford University Press, 2006.

Innocenti, Perla, ed. *Migrating Heritage: Experiences of Cultural Networks and Cultural Dialogue in Europe*. Aldershot: Ashgate, 2014.

Ivanov, Stanislav, and Theodoros A. Stavrinoudis. "Impacts of the Refugee Crisis on the Hotel Industry: Evidence from Four Greek Islands." *Tourism Management* 67 (2018): 214–23.

Koggel, Christine, and Joan Orme. "Care Ethics: New Theories and Applications." *Ethics and Social Welfare* 4 (2010): 109–14.

Labadi, Sophia. *Museums, Immigrants, and Social Justice*. London: Routledge, 2018.

Lanz, Francesca. "Staging Migration (in) Museums: A Reflection on Exhibition Design Practices for the Representation of Migration in European Contemporary Museums." *Museum and Society* 14 (2016): 178–92.

Levin, Amy, ed. *Global Mobilities and Museums*. London: Routledge, 2017.

McFadzean, Moya. "Museums: Social Mirrors, Social Commentators. Or, Who's Telling Whose Stories? Embrace Diverse Communities in Shifting Historical and Contemporary Landscapes." Paper presented at the New Times: Separate Worlds. Part of Museum 2000 Confirmation or Challenge seminar (Sweden, April 2001).

Message, Kylie. *Museums and Social Activism: Engaged Protest*. London: Routledge, 2014.

Naguib, Saphinaz-Amal. "Collecting Moments of Life: Museums and the Intangible Heritage of Migration." *Museum International* 64 (2015): 77–86.

Network of European Museum Organisations (NEMO). *Museums, Migration and Cultural Diversity. Recommendations for Museum Work*. Berlin: Network of European Museum Organisations, 2016. www.museumsbund.de/wp-content/uploads/2017/03/nemo-museums-migration.pdf. Accessed January 27, 2020.

Nye, Catrin, and Leo Sands. "UN Urges Greece to Act as Moria Refugee Camp Reaches 'Boiling Point.'" *BBC News*, August 31, 2018.

Papaioannou, Herakles, and Penelope Petsini. "A World of Agony: Representing the Refugee Crisis in Greece." In *Another Life: Human Flows, Unknown Odysseys: Exhibition Catalogue*. Thessaloniki: Thessaloniki Museum of Photography, 2016.

Papataxiarchis, Efthymios. "'Being There.' At the Front of the 'European Refugee Crisis' Part I." *Anthropology Today* 32 (2016): 5–9.

——. "'Being There.' At the Front of the 'European Refugee Crisis' Part II." *Anthropology Today* 32 (2016): 3–7.

Pappas, Nikolaos, and Andreas Papatheodorou. "Tourism and the Refugee Crisis in Greece: Perceptions and Decision-Making of Accommodation Providers." *Tourism Management* 63 (2017): 31–41.

Poehls, Kerstin. "Europe, Blurred: Migration, Margins and the Museum." *Culture Unbound: Journal of Current Cultural Research* 3 (2011): 337–53.

Rhys, Owain, and Zelda Baveystock. *Collecting the Contemporary*. Edinburgh: Museums Etc, 2014.

Schellenbacher, Jennie Carvill. "Empowering Change: Towards a Definition of the Activist Museum." Museum ID, 2017. http://museum-id.com/empowering-change-towards-a-definition-of-the-activist-museum/. Accessed September 17, 2018.

Skleparis, Dimitris, and Ioannis Armakolas. "The Refugee Crisis and the Role of NGOs, Civil Society, and Media in Greece." In *Balkan Human Corridor: Essays on the Refugee and Migrant Crisis from Scholars and Opinion Leaders in Southeast Europe*. Edited by David L. Phillips, 171–84. Institute for the Study of Human Rights. New York: Columbia University, 2016.

Stubley, Peter. "Greece's Moria Refugee Camp Faces Closure over Uncontrollable Amounts of Waste." *The Independent*, September 10, 2018.

Stylianou, Elena, and Theopisti Stylianou-Lambert, eds. *Museums and Photography: Displaying Death*. London: Routledge. 2017.

Till, Karen E. "Wounded Cities: Memory-Work and a Place-Based Ethics of Care." *Political Geography* 31 (2012): 3–14.

Till, Karen E., Emily Kaufman, and Christine L. Woodward. "Place, Memory, and Archive: An Interview with Karen Till." *disClosure: A Journal of Social Theory* 27 (2018). https://uknowledge.uky.edu/disclosure/vol27/iss1/4. Accessed January 27, 2020.

Tronto, Joan C. "Care as a Political Concept." In *Revisioning the Political*. Edited by Nancy J. Hirschman and Christine Di Stefano, 139–56. Boulder: Westview, 1996.

——. "Creating Caring Institutions: Politics, Plurality and Purpose." *Ethics and Social Welfare* 4 (2010): 158–71.

——. *Moral Boundaries: A Political Argument for an Ethic of Care*. New York: Routledge, 1993.

UNHCR Greece Factsheet, September 2018 (Greek version). https://data2.unhcr.org/en/documents/download/66311. Accessed October 17, 2018.

Veleni, Polyxeni, Evangelia Tsangaraki, and Kalliope Chatzinikolaou, eds. *Rhaidestos–Thessaloniki: Antiquities in a Refugee Journey*. Exhibition Catalogue. Thessaloniki: Ministry of Culture and Sports, Archaeological Museum of Thessaloniki, 2016.

Walhimer, Mark. "Pop Up Museum: A Short-Term Temporary Exhibition Set-Up in Public Spaces." Blog post. https://museumplanner.org/pop-up-museum/. Accessed September 30, 2018.

Whitehead, Christopher, Susannah Eckersley, and Rhiannon Mason. *Placing Migration in European Museums: Theoretical, Contextual and Methodological Foundations*. Milan: Politecnico di Milano, 2012. https://issuu.com/melaproject/docs/rf01_mela_source_book_2_placing_migration_in_europ. Accessed January 27, 2020.

Whitehead, Christopher, Katherine Lloyd, Susannah Eckersley, and Rhiannon Mason, eds. *Museums, Migration and Identity in Europe*. Aldershot: Ashgate, 2015.

Alexandra Bounia currently directs the MA program in museum and gallery practice at University College London (UCL) (Qatar campus). She is Professor of Museology at the University of the Aegean (Greece). Her current research focuses on the ethics of collecting trauma, displaying and interpreting material culture, and the political role of museums in contemporary societies. She also has an ongoing interest in the history of collections and museums. Her most recent book is entitled *The Political Museum: Power, Conflict and Identity in Cyprus* (coauthored with Theopisti Stylianou-Lambert) (2016) (University College of London Qatar; email: a.bounia@ucl.ac.uk).

Abstract This chapter discusses the ways in which museums can support and engage (with) people in need, and thus become platforms for heritage discourses more attuned to the demands of contemporary societies. Two exhibitions, organized in Athens and Thessaloniki in 2016 on the refugee "crisis," are examined using the concept of the "ethics of care." Through exhibitions like these, museums can develop new partnerships that allow for learning from the practices of others, like civil society and nongovernmental organizations (NGOs), while experimenting with different ways of advocacy. They can adapt their practices and discourses not only to respond to societal needs in a faster and more efficient way but also to reconfigure their role in society. This chapter presents such exhibitions as examples for museums and heritage institutions to follow so as to better respond to cultural, social, and political changes and challenges.

Chapter 5

HERITAGE EDUCATION FROM THE GROUND: HISTORIC SCHOOLS, CULTURAL DIVERSITY, AND SENSE OF BELONGING IN BARCELONA

MARIA FELIU-TORRUELLA, PALOMA GONZÁLEZ-MARCÉN, and CLARA MASRIERA-ESQUERRA

The Background: Heritage Education in Europe

IN THE PAST thirty years, heritage education has gained prominence as a theoretical and practical/methodological issue in the cultural and educational policies of an increasing number of countries and is the special concern of international cultural and professional institutions. This awareness among heritage professionals has arisen as a new conception of heritage policies aiming, as their primary objective, to ensure heritage conservation through the active involvement of the public. Consequently, since the 1980s, a first set of educational programs was launched in order to make heritage visible at the school level, and to make European children of all ages aware of their historical and/or cultural values. New inputs from professionals involved in heritage education (educators, curators, historians, archaeologists, etc.) began to refine the characterization of heritage education with respect to methodological issues. This more detailed concept was finally fixed in the 1998 Recommendation of the Committee of Ministers of the Council of Europe.

> Heritage education means a teaching approach based on cultural heritage, incorporating active educational methods, cross-curricular approaches, a partnership between education and culture and employing the widest variety of modes of communication and expression.[1]

This methodological emphasis on heritage education came from the expansion in many European countries of heritage-oriented projects, mostly based on outdoor, hands-on activities and on direct contact with or experience of those heritage elements included in the school programs. In contrast to the traditional concept of history teaching, heritage-related activities were and are experienced by pupils and students as enjoyable, and from the point of view of the teachers, they are useful pedagogical tools. In this way, the objectives of heritage education seemed to have been fulfilled because the programs allowed the students to better understand the different elements that constitute cultural

---

1 Council of Europe, Recommendation No. R(98)5 of the Committee of Ministers to Member States Concerning Heritage Education.

heritage by means of a positive educational experience. To be more precise—and from a heritage professional perspective—the significant learning success was the creation of a positive association between heritage and children, ensuring the creation of an active and responsible heritage public in the future.

While these wide ranges of educational activities were developed, other educational tools for heritage education began to take shape. In 1995, the Council of Europe organized a seminar entitled "Cultural Heritage and Its Educational Implications: A Factor for Tolerance, Good Citizenship and Social Integration." In this context, two additional approaches to heritage education emerged: first, the strategic role of schools as a place of encounter between communities;[2] and, second, the multiple—often conflictive—relation of the cultural background of the pupils and their families with the established concept of heritage.[3]

This first recognition of the role of heritage education as a potential political tool for fostering social integration and the transmission of values finally crystallized in the Council of Europe Framework Convention on the Value of Cultural Heritage for Society signed in Faro (Portugal) in 2005. The document draws attention to the compromise to *facilitate the inclusion of the cultural heritage dimension at all levels of education, not necessarily as a subject of study in its own right, but as a fertile source for studies in other subjects.*" In addition, it presents three innovative values of cultural heritage: diversity, cultural rights, and peaceful and democratic coexistence. Cultural heritage is, in this sense, no longer simply an inherited richness to appreciate and enjoy, but rather is an expression of rights that must be acknowledged in any truly democratic society.

These three core ideas are also present in a 2006 report written by Tim Copeland for the Council of Europe,[4] containing a detailed argumentation of the positive relationship between heritage and citizenship education. However, for our present purpose, we want to stress Copeland's reflection on the relation between heritage, citizenship, and identity. Copeland suggests that there is a common trait in heritage and citizenship, a referential identity construction. However, he states that while heritage is focused on the remembrance of origins, citizenship, by contrast, deals with the construction of a future.

Copeland's proposals are particularly appropriate as they have in mind a school population that, in Europe, is increasingly characterized by a diversity of cultural references.[5] Therefore, it is essential to substitute the monolithic and closed idea of heritage, based on a narrative of origin and prefaced by fixed patrimonial elements, in favour of a dynamic and additive vision of heritage that responds to the role of school and heritage education in multicultural contexts.

---

2 Troisi, "Schools Adopt Monuments in Palermo."
3 Copeland, "Whose Monuments Are They?"
4 Copeland, *European Democratic Citizenship.*
5 Modood and Werbner, *Politics of Multiculturalism.*

The Challenge: Cultural Diversity and Heritage Education

Concern about the relation between multiculturalism and education first appeared in the late 1960s and 1970s, associated with a new concept of the social and political role of the school that was critical of the traditional, monolithic, and instructional concept of schooling. These renewed educational proposals also coincided with the high point of the civil rights movements in the United States and the increasing immigration to Western and Northern Europe of populations from former colonies as well as from so-called Third World countries. In this context, education policies began to be regarded as an essential tool for managing the new social and cultural landscape of Western societies.

Throughout the 1980s, a substantive change took place in the educational approach to multiculturalism. The growing intercultural tensions and the low academic achievements of ethnic minority children had shown the weaknesses of an educational model based exclusively on assimilation and integration, through emphasis on teaching the local language and cultural norms. At the same time, there was a significant change in the perception of the culture of the children of immigrant families with an "increasing recognition that minorities, including migrant minorities, had the right to maintain their own cultural heritages."[6]

One of the first assessments on this renewed approach to multicultural (or intercultural, as it is labelled increasingly in Spain) education is James A. Banks's[7] five dimensions of multicultural education in which the concept of education is analyzed from a holistic, interrelated perspective. The five dimensions are content integration, the knowledge construction process, prejudice reduction, equity pedagogy, and empowering school culture and social structure.

Heritage education no doubt can play a role in all five of Banks' dimensions, following the methodological and organizational guidelines offered by the aforementioned Council of Europe recommendations, seminars, and reports—that is, using inclusive heritage content, active classroom methodologies, and the promotion of school projects centred in heritage conservation. However, is this enough to solve cultural contradictions that arise from diverse perceptions of the meaning of this heritage? How are we to overcome the existing gap between the school culture and that of each child's family and community?

Research carried on in multicultural school contexts has stressed that a non-conflictive coexistence of school and family cultures ensures not only the academic success of the pupils but also the assumption of the social and civic values transmitted by the school. For example, in her studies on minority groups in U.S. school communities, Margaret Gibson[8] argues that this climate of mutual confidence between the cultural community and the school creates what she calls "additive acculturation," by which she

---

6 Stradling, *Multiperspectivity in History Teaching*, 11.
7 Banks, "Multicultural Education," 2–26.
8 Gibson, "Promoting Additive Acculturation in Schools."

means the acquisition of new cultural competences while maintaining the family/community identity.[9]

For example, multicultural school policies are often characterized by the creation of permanent or semipermanent separate learning groups—based mostly on the degree of linguistic skill—without developing unbalancing strategies to create confidence in the students' families. Consequently, families perceive school culture as having the primary aim of erasing minority cultural identities and/or devaluating them. Instead, it seems crucial to create a solid link between school, families, and the community by means of common projects. Sharing common aims not only fosters compromise among all school agents but it also favours feelings of belonging to a wider community—the school community—and confidence in a better, shared future.

Why is heritage education especially appropriate for this kind of school project? It is assumed that heritage elements operate as symbols of collective identities and promote a sense of belonging to all those who recognize them as referential. From this premise, many educational experiences have chosen to circumscribe the concept of heritage at the local scale of quotidian life. The abstract idea of an externally established heritage shifts to the concrete and tangible experience of everyday landscapes. In this way, the educational action aims to ensure that this local heritage acquires an identifying value for the students beyond cultural background differences. In fact, various successful educational programs carried out in Europe recently—for example, the "School Adopt a Monument" scheme[10]—have followed this path, promoting common school projects for the conservation of specific local heritage elements and then disseminating their results to the wider, out-of-school community audience.

Undoubtedly, these projects have had a significant impact at the local level and have put heritage in the forefront of school–community relations. However, as we see in the case of the Historic Schools of Barcelona, heritage education, specifically on this local scale, can go beyond the establishment of these essential school–community linkages, structuring heritage school projects on three main guidelines, in a similar sense as presented by Tim Copeland[11]: first, the creation or reappropriation of heritage in terms of everyday life experiences; second, the implementation of inclusive teaching/learning strategies based in the multiplicity of competences and skills that can be developed through heritage educational projects; and, third, the promotion of those cohesive civic values, presented as cultural rights and duties, which are embodied in this reappropriated heritage.

The Setting: The Historic Schools of Barcelona

In the case of the so-called Historic Schools Barcelona, these three approaches to heritage education are intertwined: the fusion between historical heritage and lived experience,

---

9 Gibson and Carrasco, "Education of Immigrant Youth."
10 Stampa, "Schools Adopt Monuments."
11 Copeland, *European Democratic Citizenship.*

the active educational methodology, and its conception as the generator of shared cultural and civic values.

The Historic Schools of Barcelona are public schools created in the years before the Spanish Civil War, in the period that spans the decades of the 1920s and 1930s, in a context of institutional regeneration and intellectual debate, but also of social conflict and deep political turbulence during the Second Spanish Republic (1931–1939).[12] In Spain and Catalonia, institutional investment in the improvement of public education had already begun in the first decade of the twentieth century. Specifically, in the city of Barcelona, where the population concentration was very high and the need for schooling was urgent, an ambitious plan of school construction began in 1917. Despite interruption between 1924 and 1931 during the dictatorship of Miguel Primo de Rivera, the building program culminated in 1936 with the beginning of the Spanish Civil War (1936–1939). A dozen school buildings were constructed throughout the working-class neighbourhoods of Barcelona. To structure this initiative, in 1922, the so-called School Board of Barcelona (Patronat Escolar de Barcelona) was established, intended to promote municipal education policy and to enhance the schooling of children in popular neighbourhoods where public schools were practically nonexistent.[13] This Patronat Escolar de Barcelona, a consortium between the Barcelona City Council and the Spanish Ministry of Public Instruction, was led by pedagogue Manuel Ainaud and architect Josep Goday.[14]

This kind of close collaboration between pedagogues and architects was one of the most striking features of the so-called New Education which characterized the Western-innovated pedagogical currents of the first third of the twentieth century. New Education movements advocating an active, holistic, and secular pedagogy were inspired by educators such as John Dewey in the United States, Maria Montessori in Italy, and Ovide Decroly in Belgium. These approaches intended to change not only pedagogical practice but also the very school spaces themselves.[15] In Barcelona, this is clearly expressed in the school architecture associated with the buildings of Josep Goday, as well as in the rationalist architectural models of Josep Mestres, who designed the Mutua Escolar Blanquerna building—now the Menéndez y Pelayo secondary school—in the 1930s. In a frequently cited Goday quotation, this approach is summarized as stating that schools should be "palaces" for childhood.[16]

Nowadays, most of these buildings still function as public schools, preserving not only the architectural elements but also furniture, archives, educational materials, pupils' notebooks, and photographs from their foundational period. However, these schools currently face a new set of problems, very different from those they confronted in their initial years, but equally complex. On one hand, their students are culturally

---

12 Rees, "Battleground of the Revolutionaries."
13 Cañellas and Toran, *Política escolar de l'Ajuntament de Barcelona*.
14 Domènech, "Una experiència històrica de transformació social."
15 Jenkins, "New Education and Its Emancipatory Interests"; Escolano Benito, "School in the City."
16 Cubelles Bonet and Cuixart Goday, *Josep Goday i Casals*.

Figure 5.1. Building of the Pere Vila primary school, architect Josep Goday. (Author image: Enfo; Source: https://commons.wikimedia.org/wiki/File:Grup_escolar_Pere_Vila,_pg._Lluís_ Companys_-_av._Vilanova.jpg), "Grup escolar Pere Vila, pg. Lluís Companys—av. Vilanova," https://creativecommons.org/licenses/by-sa/3.0/legalcode)

Figure 5.2. Building of the Menendez Pelayo secondary school, architect Josep Mestres. (Author image: Pere López; Source: https://commons.wikimedia.org/wiki/File:IES_Menéndez_y_Pelayo. jpg), "IES Menéndez y Pelayo," https://creativecommons.org/licenses/by-sa/3.0/legalcode)

diverse and frequently come from low-income backgrounds as a consequence of the migratory processes to Catalonia during the past twenty years.[17] On the other hand, these school buildings, with an exceptionally valuable tangible and intangible heritage, are in neighbourhoods with a high concentration of immigrants and are also located close to or in the centre of popular tourist areas of the city of Barcelona. This situation frequently leads to a blurred and often contradictory identity for their young inhabitants.[18] For this reason, the educational projects in these schools have the challenge—beyond developing basic skills and transmitting the specific knowledge of primary or secondary education—of creating a feeling of attachment to and identification with the living environment and, ultimately, to support the construction of a new cohesive neighbourhood identity anchored in a material landscape loaded with Barcelona's history. These schools demonstrate that it is precisely the active conservation of their material and immaterial pedagogical legacy which makes them an example of a lived, meaningful, and inclusive approach to historical heritage.

In addition, since 2010, a number of these Historic Schools have created a collaboration network (Xarxa d'Escoles' Històriques de Barcelona, XEHB)[19] with the purpose of sharing educational methodologies, as well as promoting a common platform for the creation of cross-cutting actions. These are designed to encourage the local administration to maintain the buildings, their contents, and their history. In its mission statement, XEHB vindicates the educational value of the tangible (historic buildings) and the intangible (historical memory of the progressive pedagogy of the Spanish Republic) heritage of the schools and views them as a tool for social cohesion and a more inclusive public education.

With this objective in mind, school projects have been developed following two main guidelines: the first related to the projects' contents, aimed at the research and discovery of the schools' past, the second related to project methodology, so as to strengthen the link between the pupils and the school buildings along with their old artifacts and archival material. This methodological approach has been especially successful not only because it formally enhances the school–pupil relation but also because it has proved to be an invaluable source of information and reflection for the children. Once a school history has been established, based on the old material and archives, the project proceeds to make other discoveries about the neighbourhood, and these extend linkages beyond the school walls.

---

17 In 2017, 18 percent of the population of Barcelona was of non-Spanish nationality, but the distribution was uneven; the non-Spanish population reached 30–45 percent in the districts in which most of the Historic Schools are located: Ciutat Vella and Sants-Montjuic (IDESCAT, www.idescat.cat, accessed January 27, 2019).

18 Ortíz, "Uso de los espacios públicos y construcción."

19 https://sites.google.com/a/xtec.cat/xehbcn/inici22. Accessed August 14, 2018.

The Strategy: From Discovery to Appropriation of the Past

The common scheme of the educational projects of the Historic Schools of Barcelona in relation to their singular heritage lies in four aspects:

1. To discover the hidden aspects and to gain an in-depth knowledge of the building in which children spend an important part of their lives.
2. To make use of the preserved historical elements (old educational material, archival documents, and notebooks and drawings of the first pupils of the school) as primary historical sources so as to carry out guided research and to develop skills related to historical research.
3. To generate, through these two processes, a feeling of identification in current students with the personal and material past of the school.
4. To activate intergenerational and intercultural networks in the neighbourhoods using the school and school experiences as structural elements.

The first phase of this process is based on systematic observation of the school buildings. In this way, a dynamic vision of the lived spaces is generated: they shift from neutral and meaningless spaces to principal actors in a story with a diverse and surprising personality. An example of the discovery of school secrets can be found in the Àngel Baixeras school and its geometric gymkhana. The main idea of this activity is to contemplate the architectural aspects of the school building from an artistic, creative perspective, looking for the geometric shapes hidden in the windows, the graffiti and engravings of the façade, the furniture, the wall paintings, or the floor tiles. By means of this detailed observation and, while working on the subjects of mathematics and geometry, students also discover the sophisticated nature of their school's architecture.[20] As already mentioned, following New Education principles, buildings should be palaces for boys and girls, so architectural and pedagogical projects must be united so that their construction will be fruitful.

A second phase of the research on the history of the school involves moving from observation of the building to the direct handling of preserved school materials. The model of progressive pedagogy of the beginnings of the twentieth century advocated active learning methodologies in which experimentation, hands-on learning, and creative writing were a structural part of the educational proposal. As a result, in some of these schools, as in the Àngel Baixeras school itself, old instruments of school experimentation for the teaching of science, school magazines edited by the students, and personal notebooks of each of the children have been preserved. These materials are introduced in the framework of the educational project on the history of the school as primary sources, but at the same time, they involve identification with and empathy towards the children of eighty years ago: they shared the same space and had very similar school experiences.[21] In this way, systematic observation and research are fused with an emotional connection with the children.

---

20 Escola Baixeras, "La nostra escola, el Baixeras."
21 Cañellas, "L'escola Baixeras."

Figure 5.3. Children of the Àngel Baixeras primary school examining the school notebooks of the first pupils of the 1930s. (Author image: Mercè Garcés)

In the school of La Farigola, in the Vallcarca neighbourhood, research activities on the school building are carried out by all the students, from four to twelve years of age. The discovery of the history of the building begins with the youngest ones searching in the courtyard for the foundation stone of the building laid in 1918. This process culminates with the students of the final courses (eleven to twelve years old) developing a systematic in-depth investigation on different topics related to the school, for example, the architectural history of the building, interviews with former students, and collections of photographs, as well as invitations to historians and architects to hold talks about their school. Every year, the results of the research are incorporated in a blog about the history of the school[22] and in Wikipedia.[23] Additionally, during every academic course, older students operate as experts who explain to their younger colleagues elements of the building or other objects of the Republican years.

In the case of the Menéndez y Pelayo secondary school, the celebration, in 2009, of its seventy-fifth anniversary provided the ideal setting for the creation of a historical

---

22 http://lafarigoladevallcarca.blogspot.com/. Accessed August 14, 2018.
23 https://ca.wikipedia.org/wiki/Grup_escolar_La_Farigola. Accessed August 14, 2018. Rodriguez, "Quan la història passa per l'escola."

classroom.[24] The school is located in a rationalist building designed by architect Jaume Mestres (member of GATEPAC)[25] and built during the Republican years in order to host the Blanquerna school, also inspired by the New Education movement.[26] This historical classroom includes school furniture as well as books, maps, school writing material, etc. This space offers an ideal starting point to investigate the school's history and the history of the neighbourhood where it is located, from the 1930s to the present day. The historical classroom allows students to become researchers of the history of the school and to ensure that, through their investigation, they become an active part of its historical trajectory.

The culmination of the rediscovery of the school's history is to turn it into a springboard for community interaction. Most of the educational projects of the Historic Schools of Barcelona extend their activities and proposals beyond the limits of buildings to become central axes in the construction of personal landscapes and connect students with the social and cultural features of the neighbourhoods where they are located. Thus, for example, the Menéndez y Pelayo secondary school carries out observation work projects in the surrounding areas incorporating both the built-up elements directly related to the school and the people who inhabit and use them. The students complement their research with oral sources based on interviews with alumni or other significant members of the neighbourhood, so that they create personal links with the older members of the community. Through these learning-service activities linked to the project, the students who have become by now experts, not only in the school history but also in the history and characteristics of the neighbourhood, oversee guided visits to the school during the frequent events and open days organized by the local community.[27]

In the case of the Àngel Baixeras school, located very close to the Roman wall of the Barcino, activities have been focused on understanding the urban elements of the Roman city and their influence on the configuration of the Gothic Quarter. This work has been supported by the History Museum of Barcelona. Recently, the school community (children, teachers, families, and neighbours) launched a campaign to demonstrate the compatibility of public uses of the urban space in heritage environments. The purpose of the campaign was to ask for the establishment of a school playground on a stretch of the Roman wall originally intended to be fenced off for exclusive touristic use.[28]

In parallel, as we have seen in the case of the Menéndez y Pelayo school, many of the schools in the network are working to dedicate a space inside the building to preserve

---

24 Ara Mestres, "Una escola amb molta historia."

25 The Grupo de Arquitectos y Técnicos Españoles para el Progreso de la Arquitectura Contemporánea/Group of Spanish Architects and Experts for the Progress of Contemporary Architecture (GATEPAC) brought together, between 1930 and 1936, the followers of modern architecture and urbanism in Spain, under the flag of European modernity, with Le Corbusier at its head (de las Rivas Sanz 2007).

26 Masabéu, *Alexandre Galí i la Mutua Escolar Blanquerna*.

27 Institut Menéndez y Pelayo, "Fem Memòria."

28 Escalas, "Un patio escolar bajará de un tejado a un jardín público en El Gòtic"; Pastor Pérez, "Shaping Community Heritage Synergies."

Figure 5.4. Students of the Menéndez Pelayo secondary school during field research in the neighbourhood. (Author image: Marta Ponti)

and exhibit all the elements of school heritage. While it is important to create optimal conditions for preserving heritage, there is also a desire to visualize these spaces, by converting them either into virtual museums or into museum-like spaces that can be visited in situ. The objective of these school museums goes beyond serving as showcases of the educational heritage of the schools to converting them into living, educational spaces. This allows the children to investigate their past and learn from the history of their schools.[29] One of the examples of this type of activity has been carried out in the Collaso i Gil school, where a museography has been created by the pupils making use of QR codes. Following the methodology of the "flipped classroom,"[30] students have investigated the stories of old objects and photographs focusing on the first years of the school. Bibliographic and audiovisual resources have been used with the double aim of creating a product, in this case, QR codes, and producing material that will help students explain the school to their classmates, families, and visitors. Objects and old photographs acquire a value that they had lacked until then, since they become part of a museum that tells the history of the school and, at the same time, that of its surroundings. In the

---

29 Yanes Cabrera, "Pedagogical Museums."
30 Ozdamli and Asiksoy, "Flipped Classroom Approach."

case of the Collaso i Gil school, this part of the project is especially significant because it is in a neighbourhood of the city of Barcelona with a very high percentage of immigrant students from different nationalities and cultural backgrounds. Thus, the school becomes the basis for shared experiences. What unites the children is their school, the building they use, and their common activities. Clearly, opening it to the public expands this involvement to the community.

Concluding Reflections: From Historical to Lived Heritage

Since schools are the primary universal contexts of formal education, they offer an ideal setting for developing agency-oriented heritage projects. This has been recognized in European cultural policies and, indeed, a wide variety of initiatives have arisen in many European schools during the past two decades. However, European society, specifically in Catalonia, is experiencing fast and profound social changes that directly affect cultural issues such as heritage and identity. When working in and with schools, it is essential to be aware of these general and local sociocultural problems. Schools become crossroads of macro and micro desires and policies, of communities and states, and of personal and collective identities.

In the case of the Historic Schools of Barcelona, emphasis was placed on a school historical building approach in which pupils become active participants in the short-, medium-, and long-term changes that have transformed their environment. The "similarities" and "differences" that characterize the material environment and its human use allow children to reflect on the complementarity of these notions so as to better understand the changing relations between social and cultural contexts. The relationship of the students of these schools evolves from a first phase of observation and discovery to a second phase of research on primary sources (material, textual, and oral), and is crystallized in a feeling of belonging—the children belong to that school and are part of its history, and thus the school becomes their reclaimed heritage. The extension of this perception to the community, both family and neighbourhood, occurs smoothly, since schools are part of the everyday contexts of interaction. This is what Askins[31] refers to as "crucial scenarios" in the interpersonal relationships of the different groups that make up a community. For the staff and students, the most important aspects of the educational project are accessibility and visibility. These two aspects are related to the teachers' mission of service to the educational community as well as to the students' new sense of belonging and self-esteem. This idea is well expressed by Wood and Waite.

> Belonging is a dynamic emotional attachment that relates people to the material and social worlds that they inhabit and experience. It is about feeling "at home" and 'secure,' but it is equally about being recognized and understood.[32]

---

31 Askins, "Being Together."
32 Wood and Waite, "Scales of Belonging."

Heritage reappropriation has the potential to provide added values that are not perceived as conflictive, thus generating mutual confidence among school, teachers, and students. At the same time, it promotes the learning of critical intellectual skills and the acquisition of civic commitments for future personal identity. Certainly, heritage is about meaning, and new conceptualizations are needed to situate it in the forefront of discussion. A good example is found in the Historic Schools of Barcelona, which display a multilayered heritage by means of rigorously planned educational experiences. As Tim Copeland has pointed out, although heritage is often linked exclusively with past and conservation, in fact, the collective meaning acquired by heritage elements has much more to do with expectations and the construction of futures. Perhaps this is the most valuable idea to be retained, in the context of the future of the relationship linking heritage and local communities.

Undoubtedly, the theory and the practice of multicultural and citizenship education involve more complex issues than are presented here. They are, in fact, probably among the most crucial challenges faced by Western and non-Western societies face in the twenty-first century. But as professionals involved in the theorization, research, and management of cultural heritage and therefore concerned with its educational dimension, we think that it is necessary, for a sustainable cultural world, to base our proposals on heritage education. It is important to be aware not only of our own disciplinary concepts of culture and heritage, but also of the socio-educational research projects dealing with multicultural contexts and the promotion of democratic rights and duties. Interesting, the case examined in this chapter is a clear example of how the elaboration and re-elaboration of the concept of heritage in current Western multicultural societies escape professional and expert discussions in order to locate ourselves in what we could call bottom-up approaches as distinct from the circuits of academic publication. It is from this work of teachers, social services, or cultural mediators where we can see the construction of inclusive, focused, and democratic heritage concepts. This means using their theoretical and practical expertise from which we have much to learn.

We began this chapter discussing the Faro Convention and how it has modified the concept of cultural heritage and its relationship with people and communities. However, the educational projects that we have presented should not be understood as an application of the new guidelines and practices promoted by the Council of Europe—quite the contrary. In fact, experiences like those of the Historic Schools of Barcelona are the kind of activities that inspired the need to displace the definition of cultural heritage from what Laurajane Smith[33] calls "authorized heritage discourse," and to understand it as a dynamic and, above all, significant practice built around shared experiences and common values.

School memories do not need and, in fact, do not have to be caged in academic texts or in unreachable showcases to be labelled as heritage. Their heritage value lies in their capacity to propose childhood and learning as a meeting place and a common factor in our multicultural societies.

---

33 Smith, *Uses of Heritage.*

Bibliography

Ara Mestres. "Una escola amb molta historia." *Ara*, March 3, 2011, www.ara.cat/videos/especials/ARA_Mestres-aula_historica-IES_Menendez_y_Pelayo_3_438586138.html. Accessed January 27, 2020.

Askins, Kye. "Being Together: Everyday Geographies and the Quiet Politics of Belonging." *ACME: An International E-journal for Critical Geographies* 14 (2015): 470–78.

Banks, James. "Multicultural Education: Characteristics and Goals." In *Multicultural Education: Issues and Perspectives*. Edited by James A. Banks and Charles A. McGee, 2–26. Boston: Allyn and Bacon, 1989.

Cañellas, Cèlia. "L'escola' Baixeras: Paradigma del patrimoni educatiu de Barcelona." *El Diari de l'Educació*, November 11, 2016, http://diarieducacio.cat/lescola-baixeras-paradigma-del-patrimoni-educatiu-de-barcelona/. Accessed January 17, 2020.

Cañellas, Cèlia, and Rosa Toran. *Política escolar de l'Ajuntament de Barcelona 1916–1936*. Barcelona: Barcanova, 1982.

Carrasco, Sílvia, Jordi Pàmies, and Marta Bertran. "Familias inmigrantes y escuela: Desencuentros, estrategias y capital social." *Revista Complutense de Educación* 20 (2009): 55–78.

Copeland, Tim. *European Democratic Citizenship, Heritage Education and Identity*. Strasbourg: Council of Europe, 2006.

——. "Whose Monuments Are They? Whose Past Is It? The Multicultural Use of Monuments." In *Cultural Heritage and Its Educational Implications: A Factor for Tolerance, Good Citizenship and Social Integration*. Edited by Council of Europe, 39–45. Strasbourg: Council of Europe, 1998.

Cubelles Bonet, Albert, and Marc Cuixart Goday, eds. *Josep Goday i Casals: L'arquitectura' escolar a Barcelona. De la Mancomunitat a la República*. Barcelona: Ajuntament de Barcelona, 2008.

de las Rivas Sanz, Juan Luis. "GATEPAC 1923–1939: A New Architecture for a New City." *Journal of the Society of Architectural Historians* 66 (2007): 520–21.

Domènech, Salvador. "Una experiència històrica de transformació social des de l'administració pública: El Patronat Escolar de Barcelona." *Temps d'Educació'* (1997): 273–91.

Escalas, Carme. "Un patio escolar bajará de un tejado a un jardín público en El Gòtic." *El Periódico de Catalunya*, May 25, 2017, www.elperiodico.com/es/ciutat-vella/20170522/patio-escolar-colegio-angel-baixeras-solar-6054132. Accessed January 15, 2020.

Escola, Baixeras. "La nostra escola, el Baixeras. Text collectiu de l'alumnat de cinquè." *CCCB Educació*, January 1, 2010, www.anycerda.org/centre/ceip-baixeras/treball/la-nostra-escola-el-baixeras. Accessed January 27, 2020.

Escolano Benito, Agustín. "The School in the City: School Architecture as Discourse and as Text." *Paedagogica Historica* 39 (2003): 53–64.

Gibson, Margaret A. "Promoting Additive Acculturation in Schools." *Multicultural Education* 3 (1995): 11–54.

Gibson, Margaret A. and Sílvia Carrasco. "The Education of Immigrant Youth: Some Lessons from the US and Spain." *Theory into Practice* 48 (2009): 249–57.

Institut Menéndez y Pelayo. "Fem Memòria." Paper presented at the 6es Jornades d'Intercanvi d'Experiències d'Aprenentatge Servei, Barcelona, 2017.

Jenkins, Celia. "New Education and Its Emancipatory Interests (1920–1950)." *History of Education* 29 (2000): 139–51.

Masabéu, Josep. *Alexandre Gali i la Mutua Escolar Blanquerna*. Barcelona: Universitat de Barcelona, 1988.

Modood, Tariq, and Pnina Werbner, eds. *The Politics of Multiculturalism in the New Europe: Racism, Identity and Community*. Basingstoke: Palgrave Macmillan, 1997.
Ortíz, Anna. "Uso de los espacios públicos y construcción del sentido de pertenencia de sus habitantes en Barcelona." *Lugares e imaginarios en la metrópolis* 22 (2006): 67–83.
Ozdamli, Fezile, and Gulsum Asiksoy. "Flipped Classroom Approach." *World Journal on Educational Technology: Current Issues* 8 (2016): 98–105.
Pastor Pérez, Ana. "Shaping Community Heritage Synergies between Roman Barcelona Spaces and the Gothic Neighborhood." In *Shared Knowledge, Shared Power. Engaging Local and Indigenous Heritage*. Edited by Veysel Apaydi, 61–86. Cham: Springer, 2018.
Rees, Tim. "Battleground of the Revolutionaries: The Republic and Civil War in Spain, 1931–39." In *Reinterpreting Revolution in Twentieth-Century Europe*. Edited by Moira Donald and Tim Rees, 113–39. London: Palgrave, 2001.
Rodriguez, Pau. "Quan la història passa per l'escola." *El Diari de l'Educació*, March 3, 2014, http://diarieducacio.cat/quan-la-historia-passa-per-lescola/. Accessed January 27, 2020.
Smith, Laurajane. *Uses of Heritage*. London: Routledge, 2006.
Stampa, Mirella. "Schools Adopt Monuments." In *Proceedings of the Hague Forum 2004. Heritage and Education: An European Perspective*, 45–48. The Hague: Europa Nostra, 2004.
Stradling, Robert. *Multiperspectivity in History Teaching: A Guide for Teachers*. Strasbourg: Council of Europe, 2003.
Troisi, Sergio. "Schools Adopt Monuments in Palermo." In *Cultural Heritage and Its Educational Implications: A Factor for Tolerance, Good Citizenship and Social Integration*. Edited by Council of Europe, 51–57. Strasbourg: Council of Europe, 1998.
Yanes Cabrera, Cristina. "Pedagogical Museums and the Safeguarding of an Intangible Educational Heritage: Didactic Practices and Possibilities." *Journal of Research in Teacher Education* 4 (2007): 67–80.
Wood, Nichola, and Louise Waite. "Scales of Belonging." *Emotion, Space and Society* 4 (2011): 201–2.

Maria Feliu-Torruella is Associate Professor at the Faculty of Education of the University of Barcelona (Department of Applied Didactics). Her research is on social science didactics, specifically history didactics of early childhood, art history didactics, and production of pedagogic materials for museums and heritage sites. Since 2009, Maria has been a permanent collaborator of the History Museum of Catalonia, and supports training for educators through the creation and development of educational proposals (Departament de Didàctiques Aplicades, Universitat de Barcelona—Catalonia (Spain); email: mfeliu@ub.edu).

Paloma González-Marcén is Associate Professor in the Department of Prehistory of the Universitat Autònoma de Barcelona (UAB), and codirector of the Centre d'Estudis del Patrimoni Arqueològic de la Prehistòria (CEPAP-UAB). Her research focuses on both public archaeology and the theoretical and methodological aspects of archaeological research, especially related to gender archaeology. Paloma has been a principal investigator in numerous national and internationals projects focused on heritage education and its impacts on local communities (Centre d'Estudis del Patrimoni Arqueològic de la Prehistòria, Universitat Autònoma de Barcelona—Catalonia (Spain); email: paloma.gonzalez@uab.cat).

Clara Masriera-Esquerra is a full-time postdoctoral researcher at the Centre for the Study of Prehistoric Archaeological Heritage (CEPAP) in the Universitat Autònoma de Barcelona (UAB), and a part-time assistant professor in the Faculty of Education MA Heritage Management program at the University of Barcelona (UB). She has participated in several national and international projects on public archaeology in higher education and at open-air museums (Centre d'Estudis del Patrimoni Arqueològic de la Prehistòria, Universitat Autònoma de Barcelona in Catalonia (Spain); email: clara.masriera@uab.cat).

Acknoweldgements The authors wish to acknowledge the opportunity and privilege of working together with the members of the "Xarxa d'Escoles Històriques de Barcelona" for five years (2013–2017). We are particularly grateful to the teaching staff, who generously invited us to visit their schools and shared with us their thoughts and projects. James McGlade and Marina Picazo kindly helped us revise and improve the English version of the text. We want also to thank the editors of this volume for their invitation to participate in it and for their infinite patience.

Abstract The aims and procedures of heritage education have changed significantly in recent years, both from the point of view of educational methodologies and objectives, and from the emergence of a new concept of heritage. This concept is based on a more open, dynamic, and meaningful approach to the different communities and persons that form today's multicultural societies, as opposed to the traditional, conservation-oriented perspective. In this redefinition of the concept of heritage and the aims of heritage education, the role played by the 2005 Faro Convention of the Council of Europe is of key importance. To illustrate this new heritage education model, this text details the educational projects carried out over the past ten years in the so-called Historic Schools of Barcelona. In these schools, built in the 1920s and 1930s following the principles of the pedagogical currents of New Education, school heritage and memories are used as tools for the creation of a sense of belonging amongst their students and within the school community.

Chapter 6

HERITAGE PROCESSES FOLLOWING RELOCATION: THE RUSSIAN OLD BELIEVERS OF ROMANIA

CRISTINA CLOPOT

THE CALL FOR increased Europeanization was challenged by the admission of countries from Eastern Europe in the European Union. Post-socialist countries, once accepted in the European "club," sought the opportunity to reframe their national heritage narratives, make room for post-socialist heritage[1] in the European heritage narrative, and challenge the West–East divide.[2] On the surface, this should be the ethos of embracing multiculturalism, as the European Union's old adage "united in diversity"[3] suggests. However, as researchers have observed, although "[t]he accession of Eastern and Central European countries was justified in the EU official discourse as a 'return to Europe,'"[4] it also "made [it] necessary to re-think and re-design the EU's discourse on European cultural identity."[5] It brought increased attention to the inner complexity of the European Union and increased the need for integration.

As a number of academic studies[6] have shown, the analysis of the EU adage has not led to a clearer view of that these words might purport. Equally confusing is the very notion of Europe, as "concepts of Europe differ widely, depending on social as well as geographical location."[7] As Sassatelli aptly put it more than ten years ago: "'Europe,' as I shall try to illustrate, is becoming more and more like an icon, if not a totem, whose ambiguous content seems to reinforce the possibilities of identification with it."[8] This complicates the situation for countries such as those from Eastern Europe.

The building of a European identity (or identities), in turn, would happen in parallel with the strengthening of new forms of supranational governance that weaken the power of the nation-state[9] and enhance the hold of EU governance on social and political issues across EU territory. Delanty and Rumford,[10] for instance, critique Castells's[11]

---

1 Lähdesmäki, "European Capital of Culture Designation."

2 Clopot and Strani, "European Capitals of Culture."

3 Lähdesmäki, "Rhetoric of Unity."

4 Calligaro, "From 'European Cultural Heritage' to 'Cultural Diversity'?," 73.

5 Calligaro, "From 'European Cultural Heritage' to 'Cultural Diversity'?," 73.

6 See, for instance, the critiques in Sassatelli, "Imagined Europe"; Lähdesmäki, "Rhetoric of Unity."

7 Kockel, Nic Craith, Clopot, and Tjarve, "Heritages, Identities and Europe."

8 Sassatelli, "Imagined Europe," 436.

9 Delanty and Rumford, *Rethinking Europe*.

10 Delanty and Rumford, *Rethinking Europe*.

11 Castells, *Rise of the Network Society*.

view of the European Union as a network, emphasizing that increased globalization and mobility as conceptualized in his notion of the "space of flows"[12] can bring forth both integration and separation: "the tendency in the literature to focus on the contradictions between a Europe of places and a Europe of flows (which assumes the integration of Europe) masks more fundamental dynamics which reveal the complex and contradictory nature of Europeanization."[13] Other researchers agree that Europeanization is further complicated by overlapping and sometimes contradictory processes of "new localisms and globalization."[14]

Existing European policy supports integration on different levels. As Calligaro comments, the attention paid to minority cultures serves as "a further attempt to 'decentralize' European heritage."[15] In this spirit, instruments such as the 1995 Framework Convention for the Protection of National Minorities, "the first legally binding multilateral instrument designed for the protection of minorities,"[16] were prepared. A new notion of cultural diversity was embraced which "increasingly integrated [the] subnational diversity of regional and minority cultures."[17] It is in this intricate and complex[18] system that this chapter finds its footing, by bringing the discussion of ethnic groups' heritage to one of the most challenging EU members, post-socialist Romania.

In their efforts to support identity work and heritage preservation, ethnic groups across Europe develop specific narratives around their heritage. To strengthen group identities, they often emphasize difference and uniqueness.[19] This chapter focuses on one such faction, one of Romania's smaller ethnic groups, the Russian Old Believers. Morris aptly observed in relation to Old Believers from Canada that they "have consistently maintained a we/they boundary between themselves and surrounding populations, justified by rules within their religion, as well as by the threat of outsiders towards them."[20] The same can be maintained for the Old Believers in Romania, as I discuss later in this chapter. But first, I briefly present the group and its history, in order to contextualize the discussion of its heritage and narratives and how these reflect or refract Europeanization and other processes.

A Brief History of the Old Believers

The Romanian group of Old Believers traces its lineage back to seventeenth-century Russia, a time that brought significant changes in the course of history of both state

---

12 Castells, *Rise of the Network Society*, xxxii.
13 Delanty and Rumford, *Rethinking Europe*, 122.
14 Sassatelli, "Imagined Europe," 439.
15 Calligaro, "From 'European Cultural Heritage' to 'Cultural Diversity'?," 69.
16 Calligaro, "From 'European Cultural Heritage' to 'Cultural Diversity'?," 71.
17 Calligaro, "From 'European Cultural Heritage' to 'Cultural Diversity'?," 71.
18 Urry, "Complexities of the Global."
19 Cocq, "Traditionalisation for Revitalisation."
20 Morris, "Problem of Preserving a Traditional Way of Life," 361.

and religious life.[21] The events that triggered the Old Believer movement resulted from the Russian Orthodox Church's attempt to realign its practices with Greek Orthodoxy.[22] This followed a period of barbaric invasions[23] as the authorities saw the opportunity to advance the project of the Third Rome.[24] This realignment was led by newly appointed Patriarch Nikon,[25] who, as Stricker observes, "with no regard for church members or traditions, [...] imposed reforms at the 1653–54 council."[26] The implemented changes touched on different aspects of religious life such as religious texts,[27] but also included changes of rituals.[28] As expected, this resulted in a widespread rejection from some of the believers, who perceived these changes as alterations of the pure faith, the faith practised since the Christianization of the territory (around the eleventh century). As several researchers have noted,[29] although united in their rejection of the innovations proposed by Nikon, the Old Believers did not form a united single group; rather they separated across different hierarchies and groups. Responses varied in strength. *Bezpopovtsy* (priestless)[30] denominations believed they lived in apocalyptic times and reacted through self-immolation. Milder reactions were recorded for the *Popovtsy* (priestly) communities, which at first relied on fugitive priests, then recreated new hierarchies that would allow them to continue the practice of Old Belief.[31] The widespread reaction of the Old Believers posed problems for the church and the monarch, which officially banned the practice of Old Belief in 1666, labelling devotees as schismatics (*raskolniki*).[32]

With conditions harshening continuously, the Old Believers were forced to retract towards the outer edges of the territory and gradually moved across borders to different parts of Europe (such as the Baltic States, Romania, and Moldova) but also outside of Europe, in North America or Australia. Today, they form what Lee Silva describes as "a diaspora, although they are a loose 'federation' of distinct, mutually-exclusive communities."[33] The groups that have arrived on the current territory of Romania, mainly

---

21 See, for instance, Michels and Nichols, "Russia's Dissident Old Believers"; Crummey, *Old Believers*.

22 Lupinin, *Religious Revolt*.

23 Stricker, "Old Believers."

24 Lupinin, *Religious Revolt*.

25 Pascal, *Avvakum et les débuts du Raskol*.

26 Stricker, "Old Believers," 26.

27 Such as changing the spelling of the name Jesus (Iisus) to Isus.

28 From the basic way that believers cross themselves, to the manner in which they should prostrate during prayer, as well as the length and content of services. For a detailed discussion of the proposed changes, see Pentikäinen, "What Is Old Belief?"

29 See, for instance, Naumescu, "End Times and the Near Future"; Pentikäinen, "What Is Old Belief?"

30 Such communities maintained that since the proposed innovations were heresies, the religious hierarchy was therefore compromised.

31 Naumescu, "End Times and the Near Future"; Scheffel, *In the Shadow of Antichrist*.

32 Scheffel, *In the Shadow of Antichrist*.

33 Lee Silva, "Unsettling Diaspora," 14.

Popovtsy, migrated from the seventeenth to the nineteenth centuries to different areas that at the time were organized into principalities[34]. As Naumescu has aptly observed: "For those who survived those times, the apocalyptic expectation was deferred and eventually translated into a duty to preserve the old Orthodox rite against a world in constant change."[35] With the formation of modern Romania, the Old Believers preserved their ethnic background and, following the reorganization of the state after the collapse of the communist regime, the Old Believers created an official representative body, a nongovernmental organization (NGO) named the Comunitatea Rușilor Lipoveni din Romania (Community of Lipovan Russians in Romania) (CRLR). The NGO aims to advance the preservation of Old Belief culture and heritage. Since 2006, the NGO has been recognized as an official member of the Russian diaspora. This diversion into the history of Old Belief usefully underscores the fact that the Old Believers present an interesting case study to reflect on the effects of current global processes on this group that has created "a unique fusion of religious and social experience."[36]

Mobility and Resistant Identities

Sociologists[37] and heritage studies specialists[38] have outlined the changing landscape of contemporary societies where migration and globalization bring forth changes not only to the structure of societies but also to the inner workings of identity processes. Castells proposes a compelling approach to reflect on mobility and interconnectivity in the "network society" through the notion of the "space of flows: the material support of simultaneous social practices communicated at a distance."[39] Urry develops similar ideas to those of Castells, but presents instead the concept of "global fluids" as "entities that are somehow not simply networked."[40] His work reinforces the idea of the local, while drawing on the notion that the complexity of interactions and processes[41] can produce effects in different places. Castells proposes several types of identities as a result of the different observed processes; the most pertinent for my enquiry is that of

> *Resistance identity*: generated by those actors who are in positions/conditions devalued and/or stigmatized by the logic of domination, thus building trenches of resistance and survival on the basis of principles different from, or opposed to, those permeating the institutions of society.[42]

---

34 The modern Romanian state did not exist at that time; the territory was divided into three main principalities—Moldova, Țara Românească, and Transylvania—some of the territory forming part of the Ottoman and Austro-Hungarian Empires.

35 Naumescu, "End Times and the Near Future," 3.

36 Naumescu, "Old Believers' Passion Play," 92.

37 Urry, *Global Complexity*; Castells, *Rise of the Network Society*; Castells, *Power of Identity*.

38 Colomer, "ICH and Identity," 205.

39 Castells, *Rise of the Network Society*, xxxii.

40 Urry, "Complexities of the Global," 247.

41 Urry, *Global Complexity*.

42 Castells, *Power of Identity*, 8.

Although most of the examples provided in Castells's work relate to hard forms of resistance (e.g., religious fundamentalism), there is scope, I believe, for softer forms of resistance, such as those exhibited by the group of Old Believers discussed here. These types of identities, argues Castells, "are, at the outset, defensive identities that function as refuge and solidarity, to protect against a hostile, outside world."[43] I find these ideas compelling to understand and reflect on the situation of Old Believers.

Heritage Practices and Processes

In a previous publication, I have discussed the Old Believers' need to negotiate their identities between different levels of belonging (inner group, national, diaspora).[44] Perceived in the light of the aforementioned framework, forms of resistance identity crystallized at the beginning of the Old Believers' migration and have been preserved until today. As I discuss further in what follows, the current complex processes taking place at the national, European, and global levels have strengthened the need for boundaries in order to preserve heritage. The limitations of this chapter do not allow me to expand on multiple issues related to Old Believers' heritage,[45] so I concentrate on two interrelated aspects of their intangible cultural heritage, respectively: religion as a living tradition and language as intangible cultural heritage (ICH).[46]

Challenges Encountered in the Old Belief

Given the history presented here, it is clear that the practice of the Old Belief is essential for Old Believers' identity,[47] and community members reinforce time and time again that it is their duty to preserve this faith. This is framed in terms of a duty towards the ancestors who defended their belief, sometimes at the cost of their lives.[48] Yet the communities I visited in my fieldwork exhibited both continuities and changes in the manner in which they practise their beliefs.

One point that seemed challenging related to the practice of Old Belief was that of the calendar. As Old Belief is based on the Julian calendar, it has a thirteen-day difference from the mainstream Gregorian calendar used in the country. The use of this old calendar is particularly problematic during the winter holidays, when children are exposed to celebrations of Christmas on December 25, school festivities, and the coming of Father

---

43 Castells, *Power of Identity*, 68.
44 Clopot, "Liminal Identities within Migrant Groups."
45 See, for instance, Clopot and Nic Craith, "Gender, Heritage and Changing"; Clopot, "Ambiguous Attachments"; Clopot, "Weaving the Past in a Fabric."
46 In conceptualizing language as ICH I draw on scholarship such as Nic Craith, "Intangible Cultural Heritages."
47 Clopot, "Liminal Identities within Migrant Groups."
48 Clopot, "Ambiguous Attachments."

Figure 6.1. Religious service for the blessing of the fruits. (Author image: Cristina Clopot)

Christmas.[49] Parents have to negotiate with themselves and their children whether they will allow a double celebration in order to prevent the children feeling excluded.

The practice of Old Belief includes specific diets and rituals observed regularly. Thus, for instance, the ritual calendar is punctuated by periods of fasts, when animal products are not permitted. Moreover, weekly fasts, which not many of my informants held, include Wednesdays and Fridays as days of fasting. During these days, Old Believers should refrain from certain activities, including listening to music, for instance. This poses problems for the regular activities of some singing groups, as I discuss elsewhere.[50] The ritual calendar also regulates major ceremonies such as christenings, weddings, and funerals. Weddings, for instance, need to be held outside of fasting periods, while christenings should be performed on the eighth day after a birth.

Apart from the rites of passage, the calendar year is also marked by cyclic rituals. The two main points of focus of the calendar are Easter and Christmas, with devotees celebrating for each three days. Christmas is structured around attendance at church,

---

49 As I discuss elsewhere (Clopot, "Liminal Identities"), Old Believers do not traditionally believe in Father Christmas or Santa Claus, but have an alternative character: Father Frost.

50 Clopot, "Ambiguous Attachments."

family meals, and visiting relatives. The children play an important part in the celebration, as after the Christmas morning service, with the blessing of the priest, they
go around the village or town to announce the birth of Christ with a carol, "*Hristos
rajdaetsa*"/"Christ is born," derived from liturgical hymns. This tradition has been revi-
talized recently, and girls and women now participate as well.[51] Before 1989, only men
went carolling.

The second major event is Easter, the focal point of the year in Orthodoxy, a moment
of great spiritual significance marking the death and resurrection of Jesus. The intensity
of this religious event is marked by its preparation too, as the longest fasting period in
the year leads up to Easter—forty days without meat and other animal products, at its
most extreme excluding even oils. In preparation for the Lenten fast, requiring bodily
and spiritual purity, some Old Believers ask forgiveness from those they have wronged
in the past. Following this trying fast, the main event is the Old Believers' Easter celebration formed by a series of connected services, separated by just a couple of hours of
sleep, from 10 p.m. to 9 a.m., similar to those Rogers observed.[52] Some of my informants
made concessions for Easter, such as allowing the children to eat some sweets from time
to time or not keeping them at the service for the whole night, but this was not the case
for the most devoted.

Language as ICH

When discussing the Old Believers' language, one needs to account not for one language
but for two. One is the daily Russian language spoken in communities across the world;
the other is the scriptural and liturgical Old Slavonic. The CRLR makes full use of the
European instruments mentioned earlier to advance the learning of Russian in schools
with a significant population of Old Believer students. However, a general lack of structural support emerged at the national level for Old Slavonic.

Old Slavonic is essential for religious practice, as the Old Belief relies heavily on
the rendition of religious texts during services, by both the clergy and the laity.[53] The
situation encountered during fieldwork echoed Naumescu's studies in documenting
a community in crisis.[54] To support the transmission of these linguistic skills, ad hoc
informal learning structures were created in some villages and towns, led by priests,
monks, or knowledgeable elders. These classes most often focus on correct reading
and pronunciation, and are often gendered, although I have encountered in my fieldwork young women who studied as well.[55] These classes, reliant on localized efforts,

---

51 Clopot and Nic Craith, "Gender, Heritage and Changing Traditions."
52 Rogers, *Old Faith and the Russian Land*.
53 Naumescu, "Le vieil homme et le livre."
54 Naumescu, "Le vieil homme et le livre."
55 Clopot and Nic Craith, "Gender, Heritage and Changing Traditions."

Figure 6.2. Men reading in Slavonic during the Christmas service.
(Author image: Cristina Clopot)

do not however support the sustainability of linguistic skills across the country. In some of the towns I visited, informants mentioned that very limited linguistic support is available, and sometimes the only persons with knowledge during the services would be members of the clergy.

As mentioned earlier, opportunities exist for learning Russian in schools. However, students learn modern Russian rather than the pidgin Russian that older Old Believers speak, which has developed to include borrowings from Romanian, Ukrainian, or Bulgarian. The increased tendency to migrate from rural to urban settlements, a change of working patterns, and migration are often signalled as culprits:

> As the traditional structure of community life is becoming less and less stable and the use of Russian is generally restricted to use in the family, or possibly in the village, the young are losing their interest in maintaining the traditional ways.[56]

The researcher's considerations were echoed by my informants, who noted declining linguistic skills in the younger population. One elderly woman mentioned that efforts

---

56 Crasovschi, "Russian Old Believers," 51.

at school should be paired with efforts at home to get optimal results: "This is where education is at fault. Where does the first education take place? In the family. The family is not speaking Lipovan, Russian; they have an aversion towards it." Other informants expressed their lack of confidence in children's linguistic skills as well. "Children no longer speak in Russian with their families and the sense of language is lost," said a middle-aged Old Believer. Others shared his view, and it was linked with a loss of tradition and nostalgia. Whereas in the past younger children would first learn Russian and only when starting school acquire Romanian, the trend is now reversed. Moreover, the most recent census results suggest this: although the majority of Old Believers (18,121) still declare Russian as their mother tongue, a growing number of Old Believers (5,340) claim Romanian instead.[57]

Migration and Local Responses

The Old Believer communities also have an unsettled relationship with migration outside Romania. Immigration has become part and parcel of everyday life in many communities. Some of the Old Believers from the Danube Delta area, for instance, have used their fishing skills to gain jobs in other countries with strong fishing industries. Others have followed the Romanians' migratory trends, settling in countries such as Spain, Italy, the United Kingdom, or Denmark, becoming embedded in the "space of flows," as discussed earlier. Migration is sometimes perceived as an easily available solution to poverty. It was often discussed in my fieldwork with informants, who felt that these processes impact the sustainability of community customs in the country. In one article in the ethnic publication *Zorile*, an author lamented: "I listened with pain how localities become smaller[;] traditions tend to disappear if measures are not taken."[58] A study in the village of Carcaliu in Dobruja (by Capoți and colleagues)[59] recorded the results of such recent migrations, especially to Torino in Italy, and showed that while the attachment towards the Russian language became diluted from generation to generation, the commitment to retain traditions within the community remained strong.

In the absence of churches abroad, people sometimes resort to bringing priests over for different ceremonies, such as marriages and christenings. Sometimes, Old Believers return home to perform the traditional ceremonies, as was the case of the christening I observed. Adaptations are sometimes accepted as a result; in this event, the child was four months old rather than the customary eight days. As the parents lived in Spain, they had to wait for the child to be able to travel back home for the ceremony. Moreover, the mother was present for the ceremony, another change to the traditional practices, which do not allow the mother to participate as she is still considered impure

---

57 National Institute of Statistics et al., "Romanian Population and Homes Census 2011."

58 R.Z., "Și a Trecut Un an ... / [A Year Has Passed]," 4.

59 Capoți et al., "Carcaliu—Sat de Vacanță."

from birth.[60] These changes were accepted as natural, given the logistical challenges of the distance.

In her study of third-culture children, Colomer observes that "[p]articipants in my research feel distant (or excluded) when ICH mainly values and conveys national (past) narratives."[61] This seemed to apply to Old Believers who return home for visits. Informants mentioned, for instance, in the context of language, that children coming back to their villages spoke Italian, Spanish, and other languages rather than Russian. Such remarks were often infused with nostalgia.

Conclusion

Considering the resurgence of recent migration flows, which have influenced identity discourses and weakened references to national frames (as discussed at the beginning of this chapter) Anastasova has proposed the new label of "Euro-Old Believers," a term that emphasizes religious identity rather than any national attachment.[62] While her ideas are interesting, and may well reflect the migrants' point of view, in my study I have found limitations to its application. The analysis presented here shows that, while Old Believers form part of wider processes taking place at a societal level, they exhibit a resistance identity, keeping the community focused inwards rather than outwards.

In this vein, Old Believers' rhetoric often emphasizes the fixed nature of their heritage where "customs, traditions as well as the religious belief of Lipovan Russians, preserved unaltered, represent a living remnant, not negligible, of the old Russian culture."[63] Reflected as such, identification with a Russian culture that has long disappeared posits Old Belief as "relics or survivals signalling the distance of the present from a lost life-world."[64] The example of the Old Believers presents similarities to Cocq's study of Sámi discourses online, where defining traditions as unchanging "contributes to the strengthening of Sámi culture and identity."[65] It reinforces the assertion that Old Believers emphasize a "resistance identity" that aims to protect itself by strengthening the boundary with the outside world. Change is part and parcel of everyday life in subtle, often unacknowledged ways. But then again, as Colomer and others have emphasized, this is one of the strengths of ICH—its capacity for renewal and adaptation.

---

60 For a more extensive discussion of Old Believers' purity rules, see Clopot and Nic Craith, "Gender, Heritage and Changing Traditions."

61 Colomer, "ICH and Identity."

62 Anastasova, "Les Vieux Croyants de Bulgarie," 20.

63 Chirilă, Feodor, and Filat, *Comunitatea Rușilor Lipoveni Din România*, 47.

64 Noyes, "Tradition: Three Traditions," 240.

65 Cocq, "Traditionalisation for Revitalisation," 90.

Although Old Believers discuss cultural diversity[66] and make use of existing European frameworks available for ethnic groups across Europe, they present an example of the importance of resistance against massive forces such as those mentioned here. Migration and globalization, although perceived from the point of view of the homeland, heavily impact the future of ICH and Old Believers' heritage more generally.

As Castells notes, resistance identities provide an "alternative for the construction of meaning in our society."[67] These often resist wider narratives such as those driving Europeanization, which primarily emphasize commonality rather than difference. Depending on what these new ideas and meanings are, they can lead to subversive movements, as growing nationalism and right-wing populist factions in different areas of Europe have recently shown. They can, however, drive positive change, and this "stubbornness" and these inward-looking attitudes help communities root themselves to a place and support the preservation of intangible cultural heritages that otherwise would be lost by intensifying globalization and migration processes. With ICH practices disappearing at alarming rates across the globe, such processes are important to reflect on. Moreover, the case study presented here reinforces Urry's ideas on complexity,[68] where processes such as Europeanization do not happen uniformly and do not go unchallenged by some, where the local remains their point of focus.

Bibliography

Anastasova, Ekaterina. "Les Vieux Croyants de Bulgarie, de Roumanie et de l'Union Européenne: Identités et Migrations." *Anuarul Institutului de Etnografie Şi Folclor Constantin Brăiloiu* 19 (2008): 15–21.
Calligaro, Oriane. "From 'European Cultural Heritage' to 'Cultural Diversity'? The Changing Core Values of European Cultural Policy." *Politique Européenne* (2014): 60–85.
Capoţi, Ileana, Odeta Cătană, Mihai Culescu, Roxana Evanghelie, and Ileana Sădean. "Carcaliu—Sat de Vacanţă [Carcaliu—Holiday Village]." In *Dobrogea. Identităţi Şi Crize [Dobrudja: Identities and Crisis]*. Edited by Bogdan Iancu, 79–93. Bucharest: Paideia, 2009.
Castells, Manuel. *The Power of Identity. The Information Age: Economy, Society, and Culture*, 2nd ed. Chichester: Wiley-Blackwell, 2010.
——. *The Rise of the Network Society. The Information Age: Economy, Society, and Culture*, 2nd ed. Malden: Wiley-Blackwell, 2012.
Chirilă, Feodor, Silviu Feodor, and Valentin Filat. *Comunitatea Ruşilor Lipoveni Din România: Scurt Istoric [The Community of Lipovan Russians in Romania: A Short History]*. Bucharest: C.R.L.R., 2015.
Clopot, Cristina. "Ambiguous Attachments and Industrious Nostalgias." *Anthropological Journal of European Cultures* 26 (2017): 31–51. https://doi.org/10.3167/ajec.2017.260204.

---

66 Clopot and McCullagh, "Construction of Belonging."
67 Castells, *Power of Identity*, 69.
68 Urry, *Global Complexity*.

———. "Liminal Identities within Migrant Groups: The Russian Old Believers of Romania." In *Landscapes of Liminality: Between Space and Place*. Edited by Dara Downey, Ian Kinane, and Elizabeth Parker, 153–76. London: Rowman & Littlefield, 2016.

———. "Weaving the Past in a Fabric: Old Believers'Traditional Costume." *Folklore (Estonia)* 66 (2016): 115–32. https://doi.org/10.7592/FEJF2016.66.clopot.

Clopot, Cristina, and Cait McCullagh. "The Construction of Belonging and Otherness in Heritage Events." In *Heritage and Festivals in Europe*. Edited by Ullrich Kockel, Cristina Clopot, Baiba Tjarve, and Máiréad Nic Craith, 47–62. London: Routledge, 2019.

Clopot, Cristina, and Katerina Strani. "European Capitals of Culture: Discourses of Europeanness in Valletta, Plovdiv and Galway." In *Heritage and Festivals in Europe*. Edited by Ullrich Kockel, Cristina Clopot, Baiba Tjarve, and Máiréad Nic Craith, 156–72. London: Routledge, 2019.

Clopot, Cristina, and Máiréad Nic Craith. "Gender, Heritage and Changing Traditions: Russian Old Believers in Romania." In *Gender and Heritage: Performance, Place and Politics*. Edited by Wera Grahn and Ross Wilson, 30–43. London: Routledge, 2018.

Cocq, Coppélie. "Traditionalisation for Revitalisation: Tradition as a Concept and Practice in Contemporary Sámi Contexts." *Folklore* 57 (2014): 79–100.

Colomer, Laia. "ICH and Identity: The Use of ICH among Global Multicultural Citizens." In *Research Handbook on Contemporary Intangible Cultural Heritage*. Edited by Charlotte Waelde, Catherine Cummings, Mathilde Pavis, and Helena Enright, 194–215. Cheltenham: Elgar, 2018.

Crasovschi, Axinia. "Russian Old Believers (Lipovans) in Romania: Cultural Values and Symbols." In *New Europe College Yearbook 2001–2002*. Edited by Irina Vainovski-Mihai, 17–59. Bucharest: New Europe College, 2005.

Crummey, Robert O. *The Old Believers and the World of Antichrist : The Vyg Community and the Russian State, 1694–1855*. Madison: University of Wisconsin Press, 1970.

Delanty, Gerard, and Chris Rumford. *Rethinking Europe: Social Theory and the Implications of Europeanization*. London: Routledge, 2005.

Kockel, Ullrich, Máiréad Nic Craith, Cristina Clopot, and Baiba Tjarve. "Heritages, Identities and Europe: Exploring Cultural Forms and Expressions." In *Heritage and Festivals in Europe*. Edited by Ullrich Kockel, Cristina Clopot, Baiba Tjarve, and Máiréad Nic Craith, 1–17. Abingdon: Routledge, 2020.

Lähdesmäki, Tuuli. "European Capital of Culture Designation as an Initiator of Urban Transformation in the Post-socialist Countries." *European Planning Studies* 22 (2014): 481–97. https://doi.org/10.1080/09654313.2012.752438.

———. "Rhetoric of Unity and Cultural Diversity in the Making of European Cultural Identity." *International Journal of Cultural Policy* 18 (2011): 59–75. https://doi.org/10.1080/ 10286632.2011.561335.

Lee Silva, Amber. "Unsettling Diaspora: The Old Believers of Alaska." PhD diss., McGill University, 2009.

Lupinin, Nickolas. *Religious Revolt in the XVIIth Century: The Schism of the Russian Church*. Princeton: Kingston, 1984.

Michels, George B., and Robert Nichols. "Russia's Dissident Old Believers 1650–1950." Minneapolis: University of Minnesota, 2009.

Morris, Richard A. "The Problem of Preserving a Traditional Way of Life amongst the Old Believers of the USA and the USSR." *Religion in Communist Lands* 18 (1990): 356–62. https://doi.org/10.1080/09637499008431487.

National Institute of Statistics (National Institute of Statistics) NSI, Institutul Naţional de Statistică (National Institute of Statistics) NSI, and National Institute of Statistics.

"Romanian Population and Homes Census 2011." Edited by National Institute of Statistics, 2011. www.recensamantromania.ro.

Naumescu, Vlad. "The End Times and the Near Future: The Ethical Engagements of Russian Old Believers in Romania." *Journal of the Royal Anthropological Institute* (2016): 1–18.

——. "Old Believers'Passion Play: The Meaning of Doubt in an Orthodox Ritualist Movement." In *Ethnographies of Doubt: Faith and Uncertainty in Contemporary Societies.* Edited by Mathijs Pelkmans, 85–118. London: Tauris, 2013.

——. "Le vieil homme et le livre : La crise de la transmission chez les vieux-croyants / [The Old Man and the Book: The Transmission Crisis of Old Believers]." *Terrain* 55 (2010): 72–89.

Nic Craith, Mairead. "Intangible Cultural Heritages: The Challenge for Europe." *Anthropological Journal of European Cultures* 17 (2008): 54–73.

Noyes, Dorothy. "Tradition: Three Traditions." *Journal of Folklore Research* 46 (2009): 233–68. https://ezproxy1.hw.ac.uk/login?url=http://search.ebscohost.com/login.aspx?direct=tr ue&db=edspmu&AN=edspmu.S1543041309300032&site=eds-live.

Pascal, Pierre. *Avvakum et les débuts du Raskol. La crise religieuse au XVIIe siècle en Russie.* Paris: Mouton, 1963.

Pentikäinen, Juha. "What Is Old Belief? Who Are the Starovery?" In *"Silent as Waters We Live." Old Believers in Russia and Abroad: Cultural Encounter with the Finno-Ugrians.* Edited by Juha Pentikäinen, 11–27. Studia Fennica 6, Folkloristica. Helsinki: Finnish Literature Society, 1999.

R.Z. "Şi a Trecut Un an … / [A Year Has Passed]." *Zorile* 9 (2010): 4–5.

Rogers, Douglas. *The Old Faith and the Russian Land: A Historical Ethnography of Ethics in the Urals.* Ithaca: Cornell University Press, 2009.

Sassatelli, Monica. "Imagined Europe: The Shaping of a European Cultural Identity through EU Cultural Policy." *European Journal of Social Theory* 5 (2002): 435–51. https://doi.org/10.1177/136843102760513848.

Scheffel, David. *In the Shadow of Antichrist: The Old Believers of Alberta.* Peterborough: Broadview, 1991.

Stricker, Gerd. "Old Believers in the Territory of the Russian Empire." *Religion in Communist Lands* 18 (1990): 25–51. https://doi.org/10.1080/09637499008431451.

Urry, John. "The Complexities of the Global." *Theory, Culture and Society* 22 (2005): 235–54.

——. *Global Complexity.* Malden: Polity, 2003.

——. "Mobile Sociology 1." *British Journal of Sociology* 51 (2000): 185–203. https://doi.org/10.1111/j.1468-4446.2000.00185.x.

Cristina Clopot is a postdoctoral researcher in heritage diplomacy at the Wilberforce Institute for the Study of Slavery and Emancipation (University of Hull, United Kingdom). She coordinates the Association of Critical Heritage Studies' Intangible Cultural Heritage Network and is a founding member of its Early Career Researchers Network. Her work is interdisciplinary. Cristina has previously conducted research on European festivals in the Horizon 2020 Critical Heritages: Performing and Representing Identities in Europe (CoHERE) research project at Heriot-Watt University, United Kingdom (Wilberforce Institute for the Study of Slavery and Emancipation, University of Hull, United Kingdom; email: c.e.clopot@hull.ac.uk).

Abstract This chapter problematizes the effects of long-term migration. Grounded in the theory of migration and globalization proposed by sociologists such as Urry and Castells, the enquiry focuses on the complexity of responses to the patterns observed by researchers. The case study put forward is that of Russian Old Believers in Romania, a group whose heritage narratives echo the notion of "resistance identity" proposed by Castells. The analysis considers the heritage narratives, tendencies, and tensions observed in the community in its efforts to preserve intangible cultural heritage practices.

Chapter 7

DOING THINGS/THINGS DOING: MOBILITY, THINGS, HUMANS, HOME, AND THE AFFECTIVITY OF MIGRATION

LAIA COLOMER-SOLSONA

In short, we need to show how the things
that people make, make people.

Daniel Miller, *Materiality*, 2005, 38

What we don't feel, we forget.

Siri Hustvedt, *Living, Thinking, Looking*, 2012, 248

MATERIAL CULTURE THEORISTS engaged in understanding materialities have long explored the ways in which people depend on objects. From this dependence, objects have been mapped in terms of subsistence, technology, social relations, structures of meaning, ideologies, and embodiments, and therefore as artifacts, commodities, tools, belongings, tokens, and material signifiers. In this framework, anthropologists and archaeologists have explored "travelling objects,"[1] the "biography of things,"[2] and the "meaning of things."[3] From the late 1990s there has been an increasing attempt to move away from subject/artifact dichotomies and to understand this relationship in entangled terms, that is the embedded collective sets of dependences and dependencies between humans and things.[4] Influenced by the works of Bruno Latour, entanglement focuses first on human and nonhuman interaction through a process of mediation, and second turns into a scholarly interest on nonhumans as active actors (actants, in Latour's words): on the being of the thing, on how things manifest themselves, and on how things are active agents of social life.[5] Under this perspective things do not solely exist thanks to human subjectivity, but act and have performative potential in constructing the subject. Following this course of "thingification," I analyze things that move along with people when they are dislocated from their original homes, voluntarily or involuntarily, and

---

1 Clifford, "Travelling Cultures"; Hahn and Weis, *Mobility, Meaning and Transformations of Things.*

2 Appadurai, *Social Life of Things*; Meskell, *Object Worlds in Ancient Egypt*; Dobres, *Technology and Social Agency.*

3 Miller, "Artefacts and the Meaning of Things"; Shanks and Tilley, *Social Theory and Archaeology.*

4 Hodder, *Entangled.* See also Malafouris, *Creative Thinging*; Miller, *The Comfort of Things.*

5 Olsen, "Material Culture after Text"; Domańska, "Return to Things."

how the humans–thing entanglement operates during mobilities.[6] The things here are common and available objects that are taken rather than just carried by a migrant as "salvaged-object souvenirs";[7] they serve a role of embedding memories, creating new present experiences, and triggering future mobilities and/or stillness. Most of the literature on migrant objects acknowledges objects' roles in remembering past experiences, as nostalgic souvenirs,[8] as testimonies, or as representations of a mobile past. Instead, this chapter explores the entangled relationship between mobility, things, and migrant subjects, focusing on travelling salvaged objects as performers because of the emotional features embodied in them. I suggest that this acting of the thing is a source of affective materialities,[9] identity construction,[10] and place-making for those who move along with them.

In recent years, affect and the emotions have become a major theme in cultural studies, from philosophy to human geographical research and cultural anthropology.[11] More recently, affect has also been a focus of interest in memory studies, especially when exploring the interface between collective memory and trauma (such as the Holocaust), but also the social construction of group identity, patriotism, and nationalism discourses in sites of memory and commemorative monuments.[12] Work in critical heritage studies has recently focused on visitors' emotional responses when engaging with (or detaching from) museum exhibitions and heritage sites, as well as on the development of cognitive and emotional competences when interacting with places of heritage.[13] All of these studies emphasize the historical and cultural dimensions of affect.[14] Here, instead, I focus on its phenomenological dimension: both on the emotional memories embodied in travelling salvaged objects, and how these emotions affect (and are affected by) people to the point of performing a particular social activity, that of facilitating migrations and relocations. In this context, the affectivity maintained by the thing,

---

6 Cresswell, *On the Move*; Hannam, Sheller, and Urry, "Editorial: Mobilities."

7 Digby, "The Casket of Magic."

8 Pearce, *Museums, Objects and Collections.*

9 Anderson, "Affective Atmospheres"; Haldrup, "Souvenirs."

10 Svašek, *Moving Subjects.*

11 Affect and emotions are not viewed here as those qualities beneath the faculties of thought and reason, that is, as those affecting one's judgment (see Garry and Pearsall, *Women, Knowledge, Reality*, for a feminist critique on the gendered basis of traditional epistemology). Affect takes here its signification as a social and cultural force from Benedict Spinoza's notions of *affectus* and *affection*, that is, as the capacity of being affected by, and that of acting to. The explorations of these two notions further made by Gilles Deleuze and Felix Guattari are the common basis for developments on affect and emotions in cultural studies. See Ott, "Affect," Anderson "Affect and Emotion," and Thrift, *Non-representational Theory*, chapter 8.

12 Starzmann and Roby, *Excavating Memory.*

13 Tolia-Kelly, Waterton, and Watson, *Heritage, Affect and Emotion*; Smith, Wetherell, and Campbell, *Emotion, Affective Practices.*

14 Pruchnic and Lacey, "Future of Forgetting."

as a travelling salvaged object *chosen* to be taken when relocated, arises from the entanglement of emotions and memories invested in, embodied, and performed by it. That is, the affect stuck to them,[15] because memories and emotions of the past do not merely represent the past but *coexist* in the present through the object.

To illustrate these arguments, I use some of the objects posted by their owners in a social media project called *The Archaeology of a Mobile Life:* a stone, a collection of VHS tapes, a framed picture, a teapot, and a porcelain figure. These things illustrate the power of affect and entanglement while mediating object and people, home/homeland and migration, mobility and stillness. Through them I explore the entanglement between the travelling salvaged objects, their owners, and the migrant narrative behind them, and show how this entanglement still articulates today's life experience of homing in different ways depending on mobility/mooring conditions in the past and in the present. David Morley defines "home" both as the physical place (i.e., the domestic household) and as the space of belonging and identity at different geographical scales (local, national, community) in which people think of themselves as "at home."[16] In addition to the physicality of home, the notion of *homing processes* (or *homemaking*)[17] refers to people's affective performances in engaging (or not) emotionally with both the people and the things of departing and those of arriving, and how this is visualized in homely things. Home thus, and more particularly being at home, is a matter of affect, as the presence, absence, and performance of particular emotions (such as coziness, security, familiarity, well-being). Understood in this way, *home* is a verb rather than a noun, a state of being, and it is not necessarily bounded by a physical location[18] but defined by the interactions operating between things, people, and places. Accordingly, homing processes are beyond mere actions of making dwellings, but are also processes of identity agency through negotiated practices of placeness and belonging, positioning the self and the things accompanying it, as well as the emotions tuning these performances.

The Archaeology of a Mobile Life

The Archaeology of a Mobile Life is a social media project on Facebook that welcomes users to post "those objects that we take with us when we move, so we do not forget where we come from or who we are, and help us to make a new place to feel like at home." It invites everyone with a transnational migration experience to post a picture of a relevant object and write a short text describing what it is and why it is significant in their mobile life (e.g., the emotions associated with homemaking). This Facebook group was set up by the author of this chapter as an informal meeting place for those people on the move willing to share and explore their personal experience of selecting and taking

---

15 Ahmed, "Happy Objects."
16 Morley, "Belonging."
17 Ahmed, Castañeda, Fortier, and Sheller, *Uprootings/Regroundings*, 8–9.
18 Ahmed, "Home and Away"; Fortier, *Migrant Belongings*.

particular objects when they move onwards.[19] The group is still open, new members arrive, and new entries are posted. This circumstance makes it difficult to analyze the overall cultural creative dynamics of the social network site using digital ethnography,[20] discourse analysis,[21] or any other qualitative analysis. Therefore, and with the only aim of exemplifying my arguments, three posts have been selected. All those who have posted at *The Archaeology of a Mobile Life* have a migrant past, but only in some cases is it possible to elucidate whether their mobile experience was under the condition of transnational[22] or multiple migrant.[23] These mobility conditions are important here because they define how the semantic of "home" is perceived and experienced, and therefore its entanglement with the thing travelling along. For transnational migrants, home is that place constructed, maintained, and reenergized both in the country of origin and in the country of migration.[24] Onwards/serial or multiple migrants are those who, after a first transnational move, move to another country and adapt to new cultural landscapes. Along with this high mobility, cultural deterritorialization[25] is experienced, to the point that "home" and "homing" are performed lacking both the materiality and geography of the household. Being at home is a matter, at least in part, of affect or feeling, as the presence or absence of particular feelings,[26] and where the emotional agency of things has a relevant role. In the following section, the selected travelling salvaged objects have been organized into three different narrative sections: the "past here," the "present here," and the "future here." These temporalities are not analytical categories but frames

19 Originally, the idea of establishing this social media meeting place arose in March 2016 after discussing with participants at the Family in Global Transition 2016 Conference about how Third Culture Kids' "sacred objects" might be considered personal archaeological objects. In the world of Third Culture Kids, "sacred objects" are objects that children take along (or parents encourage them to do so) when they move to a new home (see Pollock and van Reken, *Third Culture Kids*). Since these children move several times to highly variable international locations, they tend to, first, grieve over every familiar object, place, and friend left behind, and afterwards, to find themselves lost in each new relocation before they adapt to a new culture, landscape, language, customs, and traditions. In this serial relocation and adaptation process, "sacred objects" help them to position themselves both in relation to a recent past ("it is part of my (hi)story," as they define them) and in relation to the present ("this represents who I have been and who I am"), but they also act as a mediator in place acquisition ("by putting this object here, this space becomes my new home"). "Sacred objects" thus connect worlds, as much as they remind their owners of the travels, moves, places, homes, and people they have crossed in their life. They serve alike as an anchor and as a kite of the mobile dwelling. See more in Colomer, "Heritage on the Move."
20 Horst and Miller, *Digital Anthropology.*
21 James and Nahl, "A Discourse Analysis"; Bouvier, "What Is a Discourse?"
22 Levitt and Glick Schiller, "Conceptualizing Simultaneity"; Glick Schiller, "A Global Perspective"; Vertovec, *Transnationalism.*
23 Ossman, *Moving Matters*; Oishi, "Multiple Migrations."
24 Boccagni, "Rethinking Transnational Studies"; Boccagni, "What's in a (Migrant) House?"
25 Papastergiadis, *Turbulence of Migration*; Colomer, "Heritage on the Move."
26 Ahmed, "Home and Away."

to show how entanglement not only operates in the past (that is, in origin) but also both fluxes and acts in the present and fosters plausible futures.

The "Past Here"

On April 5, 2016, Abdi-Noor Mohamed posted two objects: a simple stone from the surroundings of his home in Somalia, and some VHS recordings of his family living in Somalia before they fled. He described these objects as follows:

> I post my first photo. It is a stone I still hold as a memory and an identity for me and my family. I brought it from Somalia and have been keeping it all the years I have been running away from war in the bush and in the neighbouring countries, from Hargeisa in Somaliland, Djibouti and Ethiopia. It is the only item I managed to pick as the rockets were landing close to our house, forcing us to leave in [a] rush. My wife managed to pick a bag of family VHS Cassettes [second object posted] which travelled with us all the way from Mogadishu to Sweden over a period of three years and which we watch today in our new home of Braås.

The "past here" talks about those travelling things the emotional significance of which is related to the past. They *come* from the past, as they originally existed in the past, and their present significance *remains* in the past. They mainly represent the emotions and events experienced in the past, recalling our *origins* under the narratives of "who we were," "where we were," "what we did/were," and mostly "where we come from." Their emotional power lies in their capacity of telling (recalling) us, in today's transnational or multicultural encounters, who we *were* and where we *came* from, in a way to sustain our original identity. These are salvaged objects that people carry with them and use to reassemble memories, practices, and even landscapes in their varied sites of dwelling.[27] We may understand them as a kind of past memento on the basis of selecting and arranging personal material memories to create what might be called an object autobiography,[28] as (re)presenting distant places in people's homely environment. These objects are used thus in the present to remember particular events and/or our past lives and identity before we move. They encapsulate the representation of a past time, place, and identity. Furthermore, in some cases, as this past is lost or impossible to restore (such as in the case of war or natural disaster), these particular travelling objects "authenticate a past that is personal"[29] as much as they "authenticate" the life of the possessor, especially in the case of refugees and undocumented migrants, and they help to reestablish or redefine personal and collective origins after resettling. David Parkin states that transitional objects carried by peoples in crisis both inscribe people's personhood in flight, and offer the possibility of refugees' own de-objectification and re-personalization afterwards.[30] Actually, Parkin argues that the great leveller of forced displacement is not the nature

---

27 Lury, "Objects of Travel"; Miller, "Migration, Material Culture and Tragedy."

28 Pearce, *Museums, Objects and Collections.*

29 Pearce, *Museums, Objects and Collections*, 72.

30 Parkin, "Mementoes as Transitional Objects."

Figure 7.1. Travelling salvaged objects moving along with Abdi-Noor Mohamed's family, and posted by him at *The Archaeology of a Mobile Life* Facebook group. (Author image: Abdi-Noor Mohamed; Source: www.facebook.com/groups/1767502343538014/)

of a refugee's national or ethnic identity, or whether this comprises ideas of fixed or multiple provenance, but whether "he or she has the time to gather together enough of what is needed for practical uses as well as for perpetuating a personal and thence cultural identity."[31] The transitional object, encapsulating the social personhood before departure, is what will give her/him the opportunity of personal and family recovery from trauma when suitable conditions of resettlement allow both for the retelling of the stories that these objects contain, and for a distinctive personhood to provide for future continuity. This kind of travelling object recalls thus a tangible sense of home, physically

---

31 Parkin, "Mementoes as Transitional Objects," 312.

and temporally fixed, and occasionally both venerated and grieved. The memory and imagination embedded in this thing can help to sustain emotional relationships with distant relatives, friends, and places, triggering sometimes nostalgic stories as well as evoking feelings of homesickness.[32] In classic migration and diaspora literature, these narratives of home have been broadly explored, as they come to be associated with symbolic and nostalgic images of homeland and ancestries, origins and past roots, as well as with long-distance nationalism.

The "Present Here"

On April 25, 2016, Paloma González Marcén posted an image of a picture from her mother's homes, which is now hanging in her own house, and described it as follows:

> My parents married in Madrid in 1951 and the day after the wedding they moved to Birmingham where my father was staying with a Ph.D. grant in the department of Physics. He had already rented and decorated some weeks before a small apartment for both and at the entrance he had hung this picture. During the next 60 years, my mother always hung this picture at the entrance of the more than 15 different houses (9 cities and 3 countries) she lived! She said that no matter which other pictures or furniture were in the house or how the house looked like, she only needed this picture at the entrance to feel at home. They are already some years that this picture hangs at my house entrance—for the moment, I have no plans to move.

The "present here" talks about those travelling objects the emotional significance of which is related to the present—things that travelled along to different homes (maybe to different countries), and that help the owner to make a place *feel like home* in each relocation. Even though these are objects from the past, the emotions embodied and their agency refer to present realities, necessities, expectations, and desires, rather than exclusively to past realities. In this sense, these kinds of objects are here not only to remind the owner where she *comes from*, but especially who she *is* after several transnational moves. These things embody the sense of home the owner has experienced, created, recreated, and embedded in along the different dwellings she has lived in, and they are now acting in the present, making the new home a welcoming place.

Michael Haldrup defines souvenirs standing still in people's homes as "actants,"[33] living with us rather than for us, objects representing a past action or life, but also creating or imposing on us particular emotional atmospheres, and therefore actively intervening in our present, "making it come about."[34] Paloma's mother's use of her framed picture mediates in enabling the narrative construction of identity in her home. It recalls past dwellings and brings the stories and emotions of those past times to her new present. The thing is thus tuning her to a particular affective atmosphere, to a

---

32 Colomer, "Managing the Heritage."
33 Haldrup, "Souvenirs."
34 Haldrup, "Souvenirs," 59.

Figure 7.2. Travelling salvaged object moving along with Paloma González Marcén, and posted by her at *The Archaeology of a Mobile Life* Facebook group. (Author image Paloma González Marcén; Source: www.facebook.com/groups/1767502343538014/)

space "pregnant with a mood,"[35] and "from which subjective states and their attendant feelings and emotions emerge."[36] By doing so, the object has the power to articulate a new dwelling by triggering past experiences and memories. When the time comes to move to another home, the thing will add another layer of embedded experiences and affections and pass them into a new house in order to reenact its affective atmosphere. Across this journey, the object will thus gain new ways of becoming, mediating new experiences and inducing new affections. Similarly, Andrea Witcomb[37] describes Madeira souvenirs bought by an Australian-Portuguese family as "carriers of memory," objects embodying a lived experience rather than a nostalgic desire for an authentic experience of the homeland, or as metonyms of a touristic trip to the homeland. They act

35 Böhme, "The Theory of Atmospheres," 93.
36 Anderson, "Affective Atmospheres," 78.
37 Witcomb, "Using Souvenirs."

like heirlooms, triggering memories of experiences before and beyond the moment of purchase. They represent something that has happened around their presence, and like Paloma's mother's picture, recall all the memories of homemaking and of remaking her life in the country of migration. The object itself is not relevant; it is neither a piece of art nor a craft product, and it has no cultural connections with her home country. Rather its significance is both embedded in it by the owner and embodied by the thing every time it accompanies her to a new home. Its existence, mobility, and stillness ensure both a past and a present. Therefore, if these things are to be explored for the way they realize sensory forms of memory, then "the significance of these objects lies in their affective power, rather than in a straightforward form of representation."[38]

The "Future Here"

In March 24, 2016, while living in London, Amy Clare Tasker posted a picture of a teapot and a porcelain figure and described it as follows:

> Here is my mother's yellow teapot. She collected loads of teapots, and last time I visited my sister, I brought this one back with me, very carefully in my transatlantic hand luggage. It was a family favourite when I was growing up, and it even got painted into a mural in our kitchen in California—our ginger cat sitting next to this teapot, looking out a window at the Yorkshire Dales. The teapot has only been in my possession for about 18 months—I noticed recently it says "made in England" on the bottom, so it has come full circle (for now). Also pictured is a little statue Mum gave to me when I went to college. It says "angel of courage" on the bottom. I've had this about 12 years. Both of these keepsakes are going to travel with me to all my future homes.

Here the selected travelling salvaged thing comes from the past, embodies several home experiences in the present, and basically exists to secure future moves already imagined and projected. It acts similarly to the thing described before, but in this case the power of entanglement lies more in the future, in a prospective mobile future, than actually in the settled present. The thing ensures a life designed to experience several relocations, permits emotionally several moves to different countries, and potentially empowers the possibility of successful cultural integrations. Basically, it secures the possibility of a future because it embeds the continuity of past and present moves. Piotr Szpunar and Karl Szpunar argue that to remember and form bonds through memory depends not only on a "presentists focus" (i.e., how memory and the past are constructed in and for the present) but also on how a future is envisioned.[39] Humans extract and recombine elements of previous experiences in order to stimulate or imagine future episodes, happenings, and scenarios. In an entangled process, present visions of an imagined future also construct and reconstruct the remembrance of the past so that the imagined future has a possible existence. Using Nora's notion of *lieux de mémoire*, Szpunar and Szpunar define past monuments and places

---

38 Witcomb, "Using Souvenirs," 42.

39 Szpunar and Szpunar, "Collective Future."

Figure 7.3. Travelling salvaged object moving along with Amy Clare Tasker, and posted by her at *The Archaeology of a Mobile Life* Facebook group. (Author image: Amy Clare Tasker; Source: www.facebook.com/groups/1767502343538014/)

of remembrance as *"lieux or milieux du futur,"*[40] as catalyst elements aiming to envision particular constructed images of the future, either as utopian or dystopian visions. Using this metaphor, Amy Clare's travelling salvaged things act similarly as *choses du futur* (aka things of the future) because they project a future for her, and this cataclysm is happening through remembering past relocations and providing a sense of continuity of these relocations in the present.

Conclusions

This chapter has explored travelling salvaged things as a collection of appropriated things that people take rather than only bring with them, when they move. It has focused on things as actants in new home landscapes, embedding experiences and memories of moving and therefore creating new experiences, emotions, and memories on the move. Travelling salvaged things accompanying migrants help people to transition between relocations by embodying feelings of hominess. The thing on the

---

40 Szpunar and Szpunar, "Collective Future," 385.

move conveys the sensory and affective means of a past experience of mobility, and has an active emotional role in the process of homemaking. Of relevance here is not only the action of the owner of putting meaning-rich objects in place but also the agency of these things in providing meaning, both to each new space and to those inhabiting it. This agency of the thing permits migrant subjects to explore past, present, and future cultural identities and place affections, and by doing this, to self-explore new ways of place, negotiate belongings, and culturally self-position in each new reloca-tion. I have explored the potential of human–thing entanglements for understanding narratives of mobility, identity construction, and place-making occurring during migration. I argue here that through exploring the affective entanglement of things travelling along with migrants, it is possible to add new dimensions for understanding the mobility experience.

The materialities selected from *The Archaeology of a Mobile Life* have exemplified the distinctive quality of mobility conditions between people dislocating once and those dis-locating several times, between those forced to flee and those who plan to move. These conditions create differences in the way salvaged objects in transit define the entangle-ments of people and things, in the experience of "being at home" in the world, and the "doing of emotions" in homing. It results in different ways of negotiating identities and performing the migrant condition: connected to origins, mediating presents, envisioning futures. These conditions are not perpetual or fixed, but in flux, and interchangeable depending on different personal situations, new mobilities circumstances, and socio-cultural surroundings, as the subjectivity and identity of migrants are always in forma-tion rather than predetermined by place of origin, mode of mobility, and place of arrival. The examples have also shown that affect is a relevant compositional element in tuning the entanglement operating during relocating/homing processes. People on the move embody travelling salvaged objects with memories and emotions, and they expect that these features are (re)performed when placing them in new home scenarios. Travelling salvaged things are thus loaded with emotions, memories, experiences of moving, transiting, and relocating, as well as of being and living in transition. When settling in a new home, the thing mobilizes these qualities so the homing process can start again, and the owner can define his/her position (identity) in the new home, territory, or cultural landscape. This chapter has disclosed this action of things as a construction of reality rather than its representation, and replaced concepts of migrant identities as defined by cultural essentialities, by the affects of homing and moving. It argues that there is much to be gained from understanding, perceiving, experiencing, constructing, and enacting belonging from examining things as affective materialities, as facilitators of people's mobility, and as agents of place and belonging.

I would like to finish this chapter by adding some early reflections—to be followed up on in the future—on how the experience of migration might be conceptualized and rendered in museums of migration from the entanglement thing–people perspective. My research in heritage and mobility aims to move away from the narrative of cultural encounters (as understood under methodological nationalism), a narrative commonly found also in museums of (im)migration: cultural groups in diaspora moving and encountering other normative and static cultural groups, which are then integrated/ assimilated/accepted in more or less welcoming societies. My aims are to emphasize the human experience of moving, encountering differences, and dealing with diversity as "cultural human beings," understanding being cultural as a fluid performance, always changing, growing, and adding. The entangled thing–people performance as discussed earlier adds a dimension, that of the *affectivity of migration*, which helps to disclose cultural beings on the move. Following these thoughts, museum curatorial practices might focus both on the experience of migration as a human narrative, and on the role of things as affective materialities in this scenario of human encounters. It is obvious that museums of (im)migration have a clear social role in disclosing culturally made human encounters. The key, though, is how the constellation of encounters is set and performed, from a representational or performative angle. Andrea Witcomb says that museums aiming to engage with diversity need to enact it, instead of teaching it: "Diversity in this scenario is not something outside the mainstream, but something within it."[41] Similarly, museums dealing with migration need to situate mobility as the central scenario, not only as an accidental circumstance to those who move but also as something that affects those who remain and those who receive, and to those who arrived recently and those who did decades or century ago. Curating mobilities means exploring both people's memories, affect, and experiences of mobility, and the role of things (tangible and intangible) as performative actants in memory–affect embodiment, identity construction, and place-making processes. Museums of migration exploring these alternative narratives might help better to sustain and engage with an increasing number of visitors embodying diverse cultural identities, experiencing several relocations and sense of belongings, and living in post-multicultural societies.[42]

Bibliography

Ahmed, Sara. *The Cultural Politics of Emotion*. London: Routledge, 2004.
——. "Happy Objects." In *The Affect Theory Reader*. Edited by Melissa Gregg and Gregory Seigworth, 29–51. Durham, NC: Duke University Press, 2010.
——. "Home and Away." *International Journal of Cultural Studies* 2 (1999): 329–47.
Ahmed, Sara, Claudia Castañeda, Anne-Marie Fortier, and Mimi Sheller. "Introduction." In *Uprootings/Regroundings: Questions of Home and Migration*. Edited by Sara Ahmed, Claudia Castañeda, Anne-Marie Fortier, and Mimi Sheller, 1–19. Oxford: Berg, 2003.
Anderson, Ben. "Affect and Emotion." In *The Wiley-Blackwell Companion to Cultural Geography*. Edited by Nuala C. Johnson, Richard H. Schein, and Jamie Winders, 452–64. Hoboken: Wiley, 2013.
——. "Affective Atmospheres." *Emotion, Space and Society* 2 (2009): 77–81.
Appadurai, Arjun. *The Social Life of Things*. Cambridge: Cambridge University Press, 1986.
Boccagni, Paolo. "Rethinking Transnational Studies: Transnational Ties and the Transnationalism of Everyday Life." *European Journal of Social Theory* 15 (2012): 117–32.
——. "What's in a (Migrant) House? Changing Domestic Spaces, the Negotiation of Belonging and Home-Making in Ecuadorian Migration." *Housing, Theory and Society* 31 (2014): 277–93.

---

41 Witcomb, "Migration, Social Cohesion," 64.
42 Vertovec, "Towards Post-multiculturalism."

Böhme, Gernot. "The Theory of Atmospheres and Its Application." *Interstices* 15 (2014): 92–98.

Bouvier, Gwen. "What Is a Discourse Approach to Twitter, Facebook, YouTube and Other Social Media? Connecting with Other Academic Fields." *Journal of Multicultural Discourses* 10 (2015): 149–62.

Clifford, James. "Travelling Cultures." In *Cultural Studies*. Edited by Lawrence Grossberg, Cary Nelson, and Paula A. Treichler, 96–116. London: Routledge, 1992.

Colomer, Laia. "Heritage on the Move: Cross-cultural Heritage as a Response to Globalisation, Mobilities and Multiple Migrations." *International Journal of Heritage Studies* 23 (2017): 913–27.

——. "Managing the Heritage of Immigrants: Elderly Refugees, Homesickness, and Cultural Identities." *TEA Newsletter of the EAA* 39 (2013): 17–23.

Cresswell, Tim. *On the Move: Mobility in the Modern Western World*. New York: Routledge, 2006.

Digby, Susan. "The Casket of Magic: Home and Identity from Salvaged Objects." *Home Cultures* 3 (2006): 169–90.

Dobres, Maria A. *Technology and Social Agency: Outlining a Practice Framework for Archaeology*. Oxford: Blackwell, 2000.

Domańska, Ewa. "The Return to Things." *Archaeologia Polona* 44 (2006): 171–85.

Fortier, Anne-Marie. *Migrant Belongings: Memory, Space, Identity*. Oxford: Berg, 2000.

Garry, Ann, and Marilyn Pearsall, eds. *Women, Knowledge, and Reality: Explorations in Feminist Philosophy*, 2nd ed. New York: Routledge, 1996.

Glick Schiller, Nina. "A Global Perspective on Transnational Migration: Theorizing Migration without Methodological Nationalism." In *Diaspora and Transnationalism: Concepts, Theories and Methods*. Edited by Rainer Bauböck and Thomas Faist, 109–29. Amsterdam: Amsterdam University Press, 2010.

Hahn, Hans Peter, and Hadas Weis, eds. *Mobility, Meaning and Transformations of Things: Shifting Contexts of Material Culture through Time and Space*. Oxford: Oxbow, 2013.

Haldrup, Michael. "Souvenirs: Magical Objects in Everyday Life." *Emotion, Space and Society* 22 (2017): 52–60.

Hannam, Kevin, Mimi Sheller, and John Urry. "Editorial: Mobilities, Immobilities and Moorings." *Mobilities* 1 (2006): 1–22.

Hodder, Ian. *Entangled: An Archaeology of the Relationships between Humans and Things*. Malden: Wiley-Blackwell, 2012.

Horst, Heather A., and Daniel Miller, eds. *Digital Anthropology*. London: Berg, 2012.

Hustvedt, Siri. *Living, Thinking, Looking: Essays*. New York: Picador, 2012.

James, Leon, and Diane Nahl. "A Discourse Analysis Technique for Charting the Flow of Interactions in Online Activity." *Webology* 1 (2014). www.webology.org/2014/v11n2/a123.pdf

Levitt, Peggy, and Nina Glick Schiller. "Conceptualizing Simultaneity: A Transnational Social Field Perspective on Society." *International Migration Review* 38 (2004): 1002–39.

Lury, Celia. "The Objects of Travel." In *Touring Cultures: Transformations of Travel and Theory*. Edited by Chris Rojek and John Urry, 75–95. London: Routledge, 1997.

Malafouris, Lambros. "Creative *Thinging*: The *Feeling of* and *for Clay*." *Pragmatics and Cognition* 22 (2014): 140–58.

Meskell Lynn. *Object Worlds in Ancient Egypt: Material Biographies Past and Present*. Oxford: Berg, 2004.

Miller, Daniel. "Artefacts and the Meaning of Things." In *Companion Encyclopedia of Anthropology: Humanity, Culture and Social Life*. Edited by Tim Ingold, 396–419. London: Taylor and Francis, 2002.

——. *The Comfort of Things*. Cambridge: Polity, 2008.
——. "Materiality: An Introduction." In *Materiality*. Edited by Daniel Miller, 1–50. Durham, NC: Duke University Press, 2005.
——. "Migration, Material Culture and Tragedy: Four Moments in Caribbean Migration." *Mobilities* 3 (2008): 397–413.
Morley, David. "Belongings: Place, Space and Identity in a Mediated World." *European Journal of Cultural Studies* 4 (2001): 425–48.
Oishi, Nana. "Multiple Migrations: The Conceptual Framework and Future Research Agenda." In *Challenging Identities, Institutions and Communities*. Edited by Brian West. Proceedings of the TASA 2014. Adelaide: University of South Australia. www.tasa.org.au/wp-content/uploads/2014/12/Oishi-TASA2014-Revised.pdf
Olsen, Bjørnar. "Material Culture after Text: Remembering Things." *Norwegian Archaeological Review* 36 (2003): 87–104.
Ossman, Susanne. *Moving Matters: Paths of Serial Migration*. Stanford: Stanford University Press, 2013.
Ott, Brian L. "Affect." In *Oxford Research Encyclopedia of Communication*. Oxford: Oxford University Press, 2017.
Papastergiadis, Nikos. *The Turbulence of Migration: Globalization, Deterritorialization and Hybridity*. New York: Wiley, 2000.
Parkin, David. "Mementoes as Transitional Objects in Human Displacement." *Journal of Material Culture* 4 (1999): 303–20.
Pearce, Susan. *Museums, Objects and Collections: A Cultural Study*. Leicester: Leicester University Press, 1992.
Pollock, David, and Ruth van Reken. *Third Culture Kids. Growing Up among Worlds*, rev. ed. Boston: Brealey, 2009.
Pruchnic, Jeff, and Kim Lacey. "The Future of Forgetting: Rhetoric, Memory, Affect." *Rhetoric Society Quarterly* 41 (2011): 472–94.
Shanks, Michael, and Christopher Tilley. *Social Theory and Archaeology*. Oxford: Polity, 1987.
Smith, Laurajane, Margaret Wetherell, and Gary Campbell, eds. *Emotion, Affective Practices, and the Past in the Present*. London: Routledge, 2018.
Starzmann, M. Theresia, and John R. Roby, eds. *Excavating Memory: Sites of Remembering and Forgetting*. Gainesville: University Press of Florida, 2016.
Svašek, Maruška, ed. *Moving Subjects: Moving Objects: Transnationalism, Cultural Production and Emotions*. New York: Berghahn, 2012.
Szpunar, Piotr, and Karl Szpunar. "Collective Future Thought: Concept, Function, and Implications for Collective Memory Studies." *Memory Studies* 9 (2016): 376–89.
Thrift, Nigel. *Non-representational Theory: Space, Politics, Affect*. Abingdon: Routledge, 2008.
Tolia-Kelly, Divya, Emma Waterton, and Steve Watson, eds. *Heritage, Affect and Emotion: Politics, Practices and Infrastructures*. London: Routledge, 2017.
Vertovec, Steven. "Towards Post-multiculturalism? Changing Communities, Conditions and Contexts of Diversity." *International Social Science Journal* 91 (2010): 85–95.
——. *Transnationalism*. London: Routledge, 2009.
Witcomb, Andrea. "Migration, Social Cohesion and Cultural Diversity: Can Museums Move beyond Pluralism?" *Humanities Research* 15 (2009): 49–66.
——. "Using Souvenirs to Rethink How We Tell Histories of Migration: Some Thoughts." In *Narrating Objects, Collecting Stories*. Edited by Sandra H. Dudley, Amy Jane Barnes, Jennifer Binnie, Julia Petrov, and Jennifer Walklate, 36–50. Abingdon: Routledge, 2012.

Laia Colomer Solsona is Senior Researcher at the Norwegian Institute for Cultural Heritage Research (NIKU), where she investigates critical cultural heritage, particularly material cultural and identity, migration and memory, placeness and homing processes, community heritage, and cultural sustainability. Previously, Laia was a Marie Skłodowska-Curie Research Individual Fellow at Linnaeus University, Sweden (2015–2017) with a project on the heritage of multiple migration and Third Culture Kids, and taught as Senior Lecturer at the same university (2017–2020). She has academically published on cultural heritage and mobilities, the politics of heritage, chaîne opératoire and gender archaeology, and cultural heritage management (Norwegian Institute for Cultural Heritage Research (Norway); email: laia.colomer@niku.no).

Acknowledgements The author wishes to record her thanks to Sarah May and Anna Catalani for their comments on the first draft of this chapter. Some of the ideas were initially presented at the Museumslabor Seminar, Institute of European Ethnology, Humboldt University of Berlin. My thanks to the members of CARMAH/IfEE for discussion. Her gratitude goes also to those posting on *The Archaeology of a Mobile Life*.

Abstract This chapter explores the implications of the human–thing entanglement in the interdisciplinary fields of mobilities, affect, and migration, focusing on the ways in which it may help to reconsider material culture, notions of homing and belonging, and cultural identity. I introduce and explore three case studies of salvaged objects moving along with people when they have been dislocated from home, voluntarily and involuntarily. Through them I disclose how the entangled relationship between mobility, things, and migrant subjects might provide new perspectives on the conception of migration today. A key element in this entanglement is affect: how things on the move play along with emotions, performing, and acknowledging homing processes and mobility. The resulting reflections are intended as a stimulus to explore new forms of exhibiting the material culture accompanying mobile subjects in museums on migration.

Chapter 8

STAGING MUSICAL HERITAGE IN EUROPE THROUGH CONTINUITY AND CHANGE

AMANDA BRANDELLERO

Introduction

THIS CHAPTER CHARTS a journey through the staging of musical heritage in Europe. It draws from the experience of programmers of world music festivals and performances who work across the continent. These programmers engage with music acts from diverse heritages and contemporary expressions thereof, from rural folk in Germany and Slovakia, to ritual and ceremonial sounds from Uganda and Thailand. They also work with the hybrid tunes emerging from serendipitous creative encounters that urban living facilitates between musicians coming from different traditions.

I argue that these programmers through their activities are pioneers in creating and fostering an understanding and practice of heritage that is sensitive and deferential to the complexity of contemporary societies. More specifically, they are enacting superdiverse heritage. The concept of superdiversity coined by Vertovec has enhanced our analytical and methodological tools when it comes to the study of contemporary urban societies and the people who inhabit and flow through them.[1] Firstly, it offers a lens to explore the changing composition of our societies from a perspective of ever-growing complexity. Secondly, it gives us an instrument that allows for an in-depth exploration of how underlying and existing structural and cultural dynamics combine in different superdiverse settings, where previous categorical distinctions and classifications of social groups become blurred. As we see in what follows, this analytical and methodological perspective is very helpful when reflecting on the daily practices of world music programmers. Indeed, their perspectives and experiences allow for a privileged viewpoint from which to explore what heritage comes to mean, and what practices are associated with it, against the backdrop of superdiversity.

Building on interviews with the music programmers and on secondary document content analysis (mission statements, work plans, and past activities), my analysis reveals how these organizations work at the boundary of cultural, symbolic, economic, and social values in preserving folk traditions and stimulating continuity and change in contemporary music practices in Europe. In so doing, these organizations and their cultural programmers relate with the intangible cultural heritage of superdiverse urban (and rural) settings on a daily basis, through their practices of music discovery and renewal, through music staging, and through engaging in memory work.

I Vertovec, "Super-Diversity and Its Implications."

The Work Heritage Does

In order to understand how world music programmers work *with* heritage, we first need to clarify the "work" heritage does in a community or society.[2] Beyond the domain of materiality, buildings, and landscapes, definitions of heritage have come to embrace its dynamic and intangible side. The reciprocal relationship between tangible and intangible heritage is at the core of an approach that seeks to bring notions of heritage in closer proximity to its everyday life use *by* and *for* people and communities.[3] The metaphors of process and social action used to qualify heritage[4] capture the idea that heritage is embodied not only in objects and practices, but it is also a resource for identity building, reproduction, and change. This dynamic understanding of heritage allows us to envision it as co-constituted by a coming together of communities, materiality, and practices, and the "meaning making" that emerges from their interaction.[5] Meaning making binds communities to materiality and practices. It contributes to the legitimation and valuation of the practice at hand, while keeping it alive and in motion.[6] Heritage, thus, requires doing work,[7] foregoing any essentializing or reifying view of heritage as static or immutable.

When thinking about heritage as an active process, the role and agency of communities in doing heritage work and creating meaning around heritage and its value is placed under scrutiny. Scher alerts us to "competing narratives" of a heritage expression.[8] The protection—or in his words, "copyrighting" of heritage—might serve to authenticate certain practices and discard others. This touches upon the political nature of heritage work, whereby the claims to recognition and legitimacy of one group might affect the status another.[9] Who is entitled to represent a particular culture or heritage? Who is to grant such entitlement? Such questions lead into debates on cultural appropriation and whether it should ever be viewed as acceptable.[10] Indeed, Ziff and Rao purport a number of negative reverberations of appropriation, from damaging the integrity of a group, to distorting the nature of a cultural practice, or compromising a claim to ownership.[11] At a time when global cultural flows open up opportunities for exposure to cultures and traditions from the world over, the boundaries between acceptable and unacceptable forms of appropriation are becoming ever more complex.

---

2 Byrne, "Heritage as Social Action."
3 Munjeri, "Tangible and Intangible Heritage."
4 Byrne, "Heritage as Social Action."
5 Smith, "Intangible Heritage," 140.
6 Smith, "Intangible Heritage," 140.
7 Byrne, "Heritage as Social Action."
8 Scher, "Copyright Heritage," 453–68; see also Ashworth, Graham, and Tunbridge, *Pluralising Pasts*, on inclusionary and exclusionary borders in heritage mobilization.
9 Smith, "Intangible Heritage"; Ashworth, "Pluralizing the Past."
10 Scher, "Copyright Heritage," 453–68.
11 Ziff and Rao, *Borrowed Power*, 6.

Traditionally, the recognition of claims to heritage has predominantly been the domain of experts.[12] While identity might be conceived as increasingly complex and layered, heritage on the other hand has a tendency to remain, in the words of Ashworth, "stubbornly in the singular."[13] Hereby distinctions between authorized heritage discourse (AHD) and dissonant heritages emerge.[14] Such a dichotomy is increasingly challenged by the multiplication of entities and groups preserving and safeguarding (alternative forms of) heritage,[15] often dissenting from a predominant valuation of heritage that is anchored in the past.[16] Let us think for instance of grassroots and institutional efforts preserving popular and contemporary cultural forms as heritage.[17] The discourse of dissonance, as opposed to universality, helps to better account for how individuals and communities accept heritage differently, and how it appeals to them to different degrees.[18] Understanding the underlying power structures in heritage work requires a more fine-grained analysis of power differentials within a society, and the role core values and cultural expressions play therein.[19]

Music Heritage in an Era of Superdiversity

The concept of superdiversity challenges extant models of authorized heritage discourse in multiple ways. Vertovec introduced the notion of superdiversity to capture the growing complexity of immigrant and ethnic minority populations in contemporary cities.[20] Moving beyond the metaphor of the multicultural society, with its imaginary of collectivities characterized by relatively internally homogeneous communities and identities, superdiversity opens up new epistemological and ontological horizons for understanding the differentiated nature of the migrant and ethnic affiliation and experience. Vertovec also noted a lag in policy approaches to diversity, as a prevailing community-centric approach fails to come to terms with the stratified nature of socio-economic and cultural factors that make individual opportunities and challenges unique.[21] In this sense, superdiversity calls for a "re-tooling" of our analytical and methodological lens for the study of societies;[22] rather than taking diversity as the lens to

---

12 Smith, *Uses of Heritage*, 87–114; Smith, "Intangible Heritage," 140.

13 Ashworth, "Pluralizing the Past," 13.

14 Smith, *Uses of Heritage*, 88.

15 Brandellero, Janssen, Cohen, and Roberts, "Popular Music Heritage."

16 Hall, "Whose Heritage?," 3–13.

17 Brandellero, Janssen, Cohen, and Roberts, "Popular Music Heritage"; Van der Hoeven, "Narratives of Popular Music Heritage."

18 Smith, *Uses of Heritage*, 82; Smith, "Intangible Heritage," 140.

19 Ashworth, "Pluralizing the Past."

20 Vertovec, "Super-Diversity and Its Implications."

21 Vertovec, "Super-Diversity and Its Implications."

22 Meissner and Vertovec, "Comparing Super-Diversity."

study the interaction between communities or cultures, we are triggered to explore the diversity of diversity, introducing cosmopolitanism, hybridity, and creolization as primary concepts and starting points, rather than end results of synergetic processes. The notion of superdiversity thus sets a challenge to heritage professionals: how to contemplate and take stock of the range of diverse affiliations denizens have, and foster policies that are attuned to their hyphenated profiles?

Exploring music heritage practices offers an interesting theoretical and empirical angle through which to address this question. Music is widely seen as a resource for identity construction and articulation.[23] At the same time, "the inaccuracy of memories and narratives" can lead to a regressive approach to the music heritage of a particular time or place, favouring certain voices and silencing others.[24] Thus, understanding how music heritage is mobilized and articulated in particular places and events requires an integrated approach that is sensitive to the political struggles for representation, and where alternative public spheres that allow for dissonant cultures and identities to become manifest take centre stage.[25] The conditions through which music gets produced and reproduced are crucial to ensuring its continuity.[26] Moreover, due attention should be paid to music's sociality, particularly as it is expressed in the encounter of musicians and audiences during performances, given the important role it holds in co-creating and preserving the value of music.[27]

Methodological Approach and Data Collection

This chapter is based on the collection and analysis of multiple data sources pertaining to the working practices of the members of an informal European platform for music diversity, which brings together private and nonprofit cultural organizations from many countries: Austria, Belgium, Denmark, Finland, France, Germany, Greece, Hungary, Italy, Lithuania, Slovakia, Ukraine, and the United Kingdom. The programmers work with musicians of immigrant or minority backgrounds as well as of local origin, all of whom share the pursuit of music rooted in tradition, generally supported by the use of acoustic instruments played in traditional styles. Such music is widely referred to under the broad umbrella term "world music."[28] Yet the term is contested in practice, often receiving the critique that its origination in Western music industry marketing circles might serve to pigeonhole musicians as "other" or "exotic." Indeed, my respondents chose to refer to themselves as advocates of a variety of musical styles—and not just music that is not of Western tradition. In so doing, they aim to treat music in a nonhierarchical way, shunning an "us versus them" dichotomy which places certain Western traditions at the centre.

---

23 Stokes, *Ethnicity, Identity and Music*; Guilbault, "Interpreting World Music."

24 Van der Hoeven, "Narratives of Popular Music Heritage," 219.

25 Keith, *After the Cosmopolitan?* 58; Brandellero and Pfeffer, "Making a Scene."

26 Van Zantem, "Constructing New Terminology."

27 Taylor, "World Music, Value, Memory."

28 Anderson, "World Wars."

I analyzed the mission statements, work plans, meeting minutes, and yearly reports of the activities of the platform between 2015 and 2017. Moreover, five members of the platform completed a questionnaire in 2016, and I followed up with an interview with four members of the network located in Germany, Greece, and Slovakia. The interviews took place in December 2017 and January 2018 over Skype. Interviews lasted on average one hour. During the interviews, I asked respondents to tell me about the aims and objectives of their activities to stage and promote world music; reflect on the meaning and applicability of the concept of intangible cultural heritage to their work; offer insights into their practices of researching, promoting, and safeguarding musical heritage; and explain how they work with locally residing or visiting musicians, whether of migrant background or not. They were transcribed, coded and analyzed following the qualitative analysis approach.[29] The emerging themes focus on the advocacy role programmers play in their respective locations, the opportunities and constraints that the terminology of intangible cultural heritage presents, and how music offers a prism through which to see and explore the growing complexity of contemporary societies. I turn to these themes in the next sections. My analysis reveals how world music programmers understand the very notion of heritage and how it gains meaning in their liminal heritage work, at the crossroads of continuity and change.

Advocating for a World of (Music) Diversity

The stated ambition of the music programmers in this research is twofold. First, they are committed to making the richness and diversity of immanent music cultures of Europe (and the world) visible, shining a light on the musical specificities of the cities and regions where they are based, but also on those from farther afield. Such specificities spring not just from the migratory background of local residents; indeed, increasing attention is also devoted to local music histories and oral traditions, embedded in the memory of places and in the ways of living of yesteryear. The World Music Festival Bratislava is an example of a relatively new event which caters to this purpose: showcasing the richness of local music traditions of Slovakia and the Central European region, while also promoting encounters and panel discussions with and about sounds from farther afield. More practical sessions also cover useful tips and skills on how to get by in today's music industry, making full use of social media and online promotional channels.[30] Thus, the diversity of world music is often found very close to home, and programmers support individual musicians and communities to express themselves with music (respondent 2).

The journey into music diversity is paved with as many serendipitous as planned encounters. One common feature of my respondents is they understand their jobs as an endless voyage of discovery, combining meticulous research and cataloguing with chance breakthroughs. What makes this journey endless is the fact that diversity is not

---

29 Saldaña, *Coding Manual for Qualitative Researchers*, 1–28.

30 World Music Festival Bratislava 2018 Programme. https://worldmusicfestival.sk/en/programfestivalu-2018/. Accessed February 20, 2019.

an endpoint or a static condition, but rather an evolving process. The diversity of music traditions and styles goes hand in hand with the diversity of Europe's population. In other words, world music is inextricably linked to superdiversity, as it not only accompanies it but evolves with it as proximity, travel, and the media among others spark new sonic encounters and developments. Keeping abreast of these developments is a boundless task, which makes the world music programmers important gatekeepers in directing attention to particular musicians or styles.

The second stated ambition is to create a dialogue across cultural and national borders. Music is a very powerful vehicle to "introduce other concepts, other images of the other [...] other views of the world" (respondent 2). It can trigger curiosity in the other, helping to overcome lingering stereotypes or hackneyed ideas that no longer fit with the lived experiences of communities. This is well captured by the mission statement of alba KULTUR, the international office for global music based in Köln. "Dealing with both one's own music and with foreign music cultures helps to establish openness, tolerance, respect, self-awareness, sensitivity and the ability to give and receive criticism—all valuable criteria for a peaceful living together and the development of a vibrant civil society."[31] Central to their music advocacy role, programmers understand their activities as contributing to greater mutual respect and equality in their respective societies. Sharing information and knowledge about various music traditions, as well as bringing people of diverse background together through music performances, is an entry point to understanding each other's values. In that sense, concerts are indeed co-creation moments, where mutual "giving and receiving" are strongly intertwined (respondent 1). Performances and concerts are not only about playing and listening to music: there is a whole affective dimension which manifests itself through "body and soul" expressions and connections (respondent 4). The affective dimension of their work means that staging concerts or programming festivals is just one part of their core business.

Changing Role of Music in a Superdiverse Society

Superdiversity has shaped the practices of these cultural programmers in more than one way, as experienced in particular by those active for a number of decades. We can see this from how these world music programmers view the relation between music and the changing demography of Europe in their joint mission statement.

> The plurality of local musical expressions from here and everywhere goes hand in hand with the plurality of multi-ethnic identities that have created the new type of "multiple music professionals," combining simultaneously three or more professional activities and workplaces, while at the same time operating locally and globally.[32]

The diversification of urban populations has led to a refocus of activities of many of these programmers—from bringing diversity "from outside in" to building bridges across

---

31 Alba KULTUR homepage. www.albakultur.de/. Accessed February 20, 2019.
32 Birgit Ellinghaus, email to author, April 20, 2017.

communities living side by side, and exploring, in the words of one respondent, the "multicultural carpet of music" (respondent 1).

Besides the physical co-presence of diverse cultural groups, all respondents mentioned the growing experience of what Straubhaar would call "sedimentary identities."[33] Distant realities and music traditions come to populate the imaginaries of local residents through the media, Internet, and digitization, changing the level playing field for many of these organizations.

While twenty years ago, their role was to introduce audiences to music from outside Europe which would otherwise be inaccessible, now their role is much more about mediating and giving meaning to the encounter between cultures and social groups.[34] Given the abundance of music available online and the competition for attention in the live music circuit, they emphasize their role as guarantors of quality standards and shared knowledge and respect in diverse musical encounters. Diversity per se is not a value if not combined with a musical journey, of shared understanding and technical knowledge.

Indeed, the term "world music" tends to blur the understanding of the work that goes on in these organizations. In fact, world music tends to draw attention to cultural differences, while cultural programmers focus much more on the technical qualities of the work, and how these stretch our knowledge and understanding of music as a communication and cultural expression as a whole. The focus on quality reflects an appreciation of different ways of understanding musical mastery and standards. In sum, often conceptualized in terms of a fight or struggle, the role of world music programmers is not just about showcasing the mosaic of musical diversity in Europe; it is also, on a deeper level, about expanding our understanding and acceptance of other music canons and standards as a cultural expression and intercultural communication tool. This role goes hand in hand with a commitment to broadening the listening skills of audiences: initiating and familiarizing spectators to sounds they are unconversant with is at once a social and cultural mission, but also a necessity in terms of developing and sustaining their activities financially.

Staging Intangible Cultural Heritage

In the highly commercialized and competitive field of live music, world music is arguably relatively niche. This poses a number of challenges: first, there is pressure to fill the room and to appeal to a wider audience and develop wider market shares. Given its inherent variety, a world music program is likely to attract varying levels of attention, and having at least some degree of familiarity with the music tends to guarantee a higher level of visibility and attendance. Indeed, programmers notice how part of the audiences share an ethnic or national bond with the musicians on stage, often making visible local communities and groups which were previously unnoticed (respondents 1 and 2). Programmers engage in the study and dissemination of information and background knowledge of

---

33 Straubhaar, "Mapping 'Global.'"
34 See Brandellero and Kloosterman, "More Than Just Bytes."

the musicians they work with, guiding their audiences though a culture switch that will allow for deeper understanding of the musical form and experience.

Second, programmers feel the squeeze from more mainstream genres, which are "safer bets" for venues looking for higher ticket sales and consumptions. As a result, there is a perception that the number of venues is getting sparser, while commercial pressure is getting higher, including on public spaces, where the need to pay for permits and rents is now the rule rather than the exception.

To respond to this "double pinch" of sparser venues and commercialization, cultural programmers have over the years developed their own meeting points, events, collaborations, and festivals. Festivals such as WOMAD provide opportunities to meet kindred spirits and network. Unlike other music genres, such as jazz or classical music, world music is not highly institutionalized. A lack of infrastructure means that initiatives such as joint tours of festivals are mostly planned from the bottom up. Fostering and supporting artistic mobility across Europe through programmes of exchange gains twofold relevance. Firstly, it is a way of broadening the public and visibility for specific music forms. Secondly, it is a way of stimulating encounters and cross-fertilization, which in turn can light a spark of creativity engendering novel hybrid sounds, or simply new contexts in which music can be appreciated under a new light (respondent 2).

Dealing with Continuity and Change

World music cultural programmers often find themselves in a liminal position, at the boundary of continuity and change, as they work with traditional music, folk, and contemporary musical expressions of the world, helping to create new sounds along the way. The terminology of intangible cultural heritage opens up opportunities to signal an "extra" layer of value of certain musicians and traditions, yet it also poses certain dilemmas. Indeed, when explaining how the notion of intangible cultural heritage comes to shape their own daily practices, two aspects emerge: on one hand, there is the formal notion of music that has been granted recognition by UNESCO. While programmers do work and stage such music traditions, they are by no means the only form of music they deal with and might even be marginal to their practices. Moreover, UNESCO recognition might entail a certain level of institutionalization that counters the grassroots nature of much of the programmers' work. More broadly speaking, therefore, programmers work with notions of intangible cultural heritage that consider music traditions as a living practice (as opposed to a preserved fixed cultural form). Staging living practices requires an understanding of how people are using cultural expressions in their daily lives, so that a performance does not result in a spectacle void of meaning and emotive attachment. Programmers see their role as one of supporting and facilitating the living manifestation of music traditions in the communities' own terms and in the terms of those communities with which such traditions resonate. In particular, one programmer noted a thirst for roots, particularly among urban dwellers: "a lot of people in the big cities are looking forward to finding these ways back to the roots. It's amazing how many people are making instruments or how many people learn to make some or [...] use these products in a new way" (respondent 3).

The notion of "own terms" in fact comes with a caveat: ownership is a disputed concept in this circle. The Greek organization En Chordais, for instance, sees its work as focusing on the musical traditions of the Mediterranean region, from the southern Balkan countries to Persian and Armenian traditions.[35] While this modal music has roots in Greece, its historic trans-local influences and exchanges with the wider region are undisputed. This emphasis on long-standing contacts and exchanges between music traditions results in an approach to traditions which places emphasis on their relations and their past and contemporary dialogues, rather than on their distinctions and separations. Music traditions are acknowledged as being hybrid, the result of centuries of contacts and exchanges. Such curiosity and exchange is also a prerogative of contemporary artists. "The artists are curious, they want to try out new stuff, they should do it! [...] Culture and music is living, it's a living tradition, it has to expand, exchange, we have to meet musicians, musicians have to meet. That's what we try to have to achieve intangible music" (respondent 2).

Moreover, the notion of ownership places the onus of preservation onto specific communities, who are not always in a condition to support the continuity of their own tradition, due to wider political turmoil or dwindling attention among younger generations. Van Zantem writes that culture "can only have continuity if people enjoy the conditions to produce and re-create it."[36] Yet is it clear that conditions play only a part in this process: reflecting on the continuity of certain traditions also calls us to reflect on the meanings attached with kindling traditions and how such meanings might change through time and generations. As a result, one programmer also questioned the implicit value bias towards more static music styles: "so people in Papua New Guinea they have new video and mobile phones [...] they listen to music from all over the world if they like. So [protecting traditions], it's somehow putting something under glass [...] of course they should be proud of what they are doing but they should also be able to if they are interested in exchanging with others, getting to know other concepts of music [...], giving and passing over the richness to others" (respondent 2).

Working with the concept of intangible cultural heritage thus results in a different set of practices. The first relates to approaches to supporting living music traditions. Cultural programmers make sense of their own daily practices by keeping memories of knowledge and identities alive through music, poetry, or oral traditions, for instance. Most respondents are sure to state clearly that they include new musical forms that give identity and engage with aspects of the daily life of communities. They understand the protection and preservation of music as a practice that does not attempt to freeze a practice in time. Indeed, one metaphor described tradition as a moving line stretching from the present to the past and into the future, a line on which it is practically impossible to stand still. This seems also crucial in attracting younger generations to the practice and transmission of cultural practices in a way that is relevant to contemporary society.

---

35 En Chordais. www.facebook.com/pg/En-Chordais-%CE%95%CE%BD-%CE%A7%CE%BF%CF%81%CE%B4%CE%B1%CE%AF%CF%82-231723267948/about/. Accessed February 20, 2019.
36 Van Zantem, "Constructing New Terminology," 37.

At the same time, even when a tradition line is broken and it is no longer practised or being kept alive, dialogue and exchange can help to reactivate a cultural form. Another powerful metaphor was used in one of the interviews to describe this process: let us think of the forest floor, where from past trees and leaves, new shoots and plants can flourish. In this metaphor, the role of passing the baton and bringing back to life a tradition does not always and necessarily take place within the original social group. Indeed, musicians and communities whose music and spirit resonates with the lost or dying tradition have played an important role in bringing it back to life.

The work programmers themselves do in terms of cataloguing and recording tradition is paramount to a deep understanding of place and its history. But preserving the memory of music is not the ultimate goal for the programmers I spoke to. One respondent said he was not "the one looking back" (respondent 2). Efforts to record and classify music, such as the work done by the Smithsonian with its Folkway recordings and magazines, are seen as extremely laudable. Yet that is only one part of the process.

Conclusions

Superdiversity challenges us to find new ways of conceptualizing heritage in contemporary urban society, taking into account the complex state of continuous multi-layering of existing and newly arriving populations.[37]

From their—as they state—privileged position at the hub of a network of worldwide music flows, world music programmers are increasingly engaged with the production of hybrid sonic expressions of a superdiverse European population.[38] Based on their own knowledge and network, the programmers function as makers and enactors of superdiversity, by actively encouraging and promoting encounters across social groups and musical exchanges between musicians with different skills and practices, that in turn might result in hybrid new sounds, musical experiences, or recordings. While not wanting to instrumentalize culture, these musical encounters offer good examples of how peaceful and respectful cohabitation of different cultures can happen and can lead to deep connections between groups, working together to achieve something that is unique and innovative. Their work offers insights into how to "pluralize" heritage of contemporary urban societies.[39]

By striking a balance between a deep respect of traditions and their potential for innovation and relevance to present-day societies, the practices of world music programmers offer insights and learning points on how to resolve the tension between continuity and change. In the way these programmers tell us about the sounds of Europe and the world, they also tell us about the story of our contemporary society, how it connects to its past and what the future might hold. They are an embodiment of the goals of bringing people together, strengthening the ties between people and societies.

---

37 Grzymala-Kazlowska and Phillimore, "Introduction: Rethinking Integration."

38 Brandellero and Pfeffer, "Multiple and Shifting Geographies of World Music."

39 Ashworth, "Pluralizing the Past."

Bibliography

Anderson, Ian. "World Wars." www.ianaanderson.com/world-music/. Accessed May 29, 2017.
Ashworth, Gregory J. "Pluralizing the Past: Heritage Policies in Plural Societies." *Edinburgh Architecture Research* 30 (2006): 13–23.
Ashworth, Gregory J., Graham Brian, and John E. Tunbridge. *Pluralising Pasts: Heritage, Identity and Place in Multicultural Societies.* London: Pluto, 2007.
Brandellero, Amanda. "Multiple and Shifting Geographies of World Music Production." *Area* 43 (2011): 495–505.
Brandellero, Amanda, and Robert Kloosterman. "More Than Just Bytes: The Paris Cluster of World Music Production." In *The Production and Consumption of Music in the Digital Age.* Edited by Brian Hracs, Michael Seman, and Tarek Virani, 177–89. London: Routledge, 2016.
Brandellero, Amanda, Susanne Janssen, Sara Cohen, and Les Roberts. "Popular Music Heritage, Cultural Memory and Cultural Identity." *International Journal of Heritage Studies* 20 (2014): 219–23.
Brandellero, Amanda, Susanne Janssen, Sara Cohen, Les Roberts, and Karin Pfeffer. "Making a Scene: Geographies of Music Scenes in The Netherlands 1965–2010." *Environment and Planning A* 47 (2015): 1574–91.
Byrne, Denis. "Heritage as Social Action." In *The Heritage Reader.* Edited by Graham Fairclough, Rodney Harrison, John H. Jameson Jr., and John Schofield, 149–73. Abingdon: Routledge, 2008.
Guilbault, Jocelyne. "Interpreting World Music: A Challenge in Theory and Practice." *Popular Music* 16 (1997): 31–44.
Grzymala-Kazlowska, Aleksandra, and Phillimore Jenny. "Introduction: Rethinking Integration: New Perspectives on Adaptation and Settlement in the Era of Super-diversity." *Journal of Ethnic and Migration Studies* 44 (2018): 179–96.
Hall, Stuart. "Whose Heritage? Un-settling 'The Heritage,' Re-imagining it Post-nation." *Third Text* 49 (1999): 3–13.
Keith, Michael. *After the Cosmopolitan? Multicultural Cities and the Future of Racism.* London: Routledge, 2005.
Kirshenblatt-Gimblett, Barbara. "Intangible Heritage as Metacultural Production." *Museum International* 56 (2004): 52–65.
Lixinski, Lucas. "Selecting Heritage: The Interplay of Art, Politics and Identity." *European Journal of International Law* 22 (2011): 81–100.
Meissner, Fran, and Vertovec Steven. "Comparing Super-Diversity." *Ethnic and Racial Studies* 38 (2015): 541–55.
Munjeri, Dawson. "Tangible and Intangible Heritage: From Difference to Convergence." *Museum International* 56 (2004): 12–20.
Saldaña, Johnny. *The Coding Manual for Qualitative Researchers*, 1–303. London: Sage, 2016.
Scher, Philip W. "Copyright Heritage: Preservation, Carnival and the State in Trinidad." *Anthropological Quarterly* 75 (2002): 453–84.
Smith, Laurajane. "Intangible Heritage: A Challenge to the Authorised Heritage Discourse?" *Revista de Etnologia de Cataluña* 40 (2015): 133–42.
——. *Uses of Heritage.* London: Routledge, 2006.
Stokes, Martin. *Ethnicity, Identity and Music: The Musical Construction of Place.* Oxford: Berg, 1994.
Straubhaar, Joseph D. "Mapping 'Global' in Global Communication and Media Studies." In *Global Communication: New Agendas in Communication.* Edited by Karin G. Wilkins, Joseph D. Straubhaar, and Shanti Kumar, 10–34. London: Routledge, 2014.

Taylor, Timothy. "World Music, Value, Memory." In *Speaking in Tongues: Pop, Lokal, Global.* Edited by Dietrich Helms and Thomas Phelps, 103–17. Bielefeld: Transcript, 2015.

Van der Hoeven, Arno. "Narratives of Popular Music Heritage and Cultural Identity: The Affordances and Constraints of Popular Music Memories." *European Journal of Cultural Studies* 21 (2018): 207–22.

Van Zanten, Wim. "Constructing New Terminology for Intangible Cultural Heritage." *Museum International* 56 (2004): 36–44.

Vertovec, Steven. "Super-Diversity and Its Implications." *Ethnic and Racial Studies* 30(2007): 1024–54.

Ziff, Bruce, and Pratima Rao. *Borrowed Power: Essays on Cultural Appropriation.* New Brunswick: Rutgers University Press, 1997.

Amanda Brandellero is Assistant Professor at the Erasmus School of History, Culture and Communication, Erasmus University Rotterdam, The Netherlands. Her research explores how cultural production, consumption, and heritage in urban settings are shaped by globalization and the experience of interconnectedness with flows of people, products, and media. Her research has taken a comparative approach, with case studies in different contemporary European settings and Brazil. Amanda has also researched different cultural and creative industries, including popular music and contemporary art (Department of Arts and Culture, Erasmus University Rotterdam, The Netherlands; email: Brandellero@eshcc.eur.nl).

Acknowledgements I would like to record my thanks to participants of the international UNESCO conference "Urban Cultures, Superdiversity and Intangible Heritage," held in Utrecht on February 15, 2018, for their insights and suggestions. I thank my respondents for their time and commitment.

Abstract This chapter addresses the challenges and opportunities faced by promoters of festivals and performances when staging music acts from diverse musical heritages in Europe. I explore the working practices of world music programmers, exploring their role as makers and enactors of music superdiversity in Europe. In their daily practices, they actively encourage and promote encounters across social groups and musical exchanges between musicians with different skills and traditions. Building on interviews with the organizations' directors and on secondary document content analysis (mission statements, work plans, and past activities), my analysis reveals how these organizations work at the boundary of cultural, symbolic, economic, and social values in preserving folk traditions and stimulating more contemporary world music. This chapter concludes with some directions on how the tension between social, cultural-symbolic, and economic values can be resolved in order to support music's empowering role in diverse communities, as well as its catalyzing function in bringing people together.

Afterword

SUPERDIVERSITY AND NEW APPROACHES TO HERITAGE AND IDENTITIES IN EUROPE: THE WAY FORWARD

SOPHIA LABADI

THIS VOLUME IS rich in its diversity of themes, including museum theatre by refugee artists, museum activism, heritage and multicultural education, musical heritage, and individual cultural identity. In covering such a variety of areas, this book has pushed boundaries and contributed to our understanding of how superdiversity encourages new approaches to cultural heritage and identities in Europe. This afterword cannot cover all the diverse themes in this volume. Instead, I concentrate on a critical discussion of some issues raised here that resonate with my own research on the topic of cultural organizations and (im)migrants and some of my work in the field.[1]

Several chapters in this volume have detailed the need for cultural organizations to reform themselves in order to reflect more comprehensively the concept of superdiversity and its effect on cultural identities and heritage. The chapters by Bounia and Jeffers clearly articulate a way for cultural organizations and museums to engage more effectively with contemporary societal issues. Manchester Museum, as explained in Jeffers's chapter, has successfully embraced a model of active engagement with current affairs through regular work with refugee and migrant artists, including the staging of refugee theatre plays in its galleries. However, the willingness of some museums to engage fully with current affairs does not mean that all institutions have adopted such a stance. In my research, I have documented the reluctance of some cultural organizations to engage with such topics, especially sensitive political issues such as those relating to refugees and (im)migrants. One example is the National Museum on the History of Immigration in Paris (Musée National de l'Histoire de l'Immigration), which considers (im)migration a historical phenomenon rather than a contemporary one. It aims to be "apolitical" and neutral in order to attract as wide a public as possible.[2] These examples reflect differing models, with Manchester Museum being a free and popular museum whilst the Paris museum is a fee-paying institution with reduced public funding and a limited audience. The Paris museum is perhaps careful to curate an apolitical narrative in order not to alienate its already small audience. Current affairs can lead to heated debates, because of their increased temporal proximity and emotional resonance when compared with historical events. Many museums would therefore see an engagement with current affairs as undermining their credibility, even their very definition, as temples of "objectivity" and "neutrality." These institutions need to rethink their role in society and, if they take their role as agents of social change seriously, they do need to engage more actively with ongoing societal issues.

---

1 Labadi, *Museums, Immigrants, and Social Justice*; Labadi, "National Museum."

2 Labadi, *Museums, Immigrants, and Social Justice*, 53.

Cultural organizations can reflect superdiverse societies more fully if they organize programs beyond their physical boundaries and thus become "institutions without walls." Bounia's chapter illustrates how this could happen, with exhibitions in the form of posters displayed at bus and tram stops, inside metro stations, and on trains around Athens, to celebrate the solidarity of the Greek people with refugee and migrant communities in 2016. Working beyond their walls enables cultural institutions to target not only their existing audience, who might already have positive views on immigration phenomena, but also a broader audience who might have negative opinions of (im)migrants and refugees. These innovative approaches should be multiplied to ensure that cultural institutions have a wider impact on public opinion regarding the xenophobic narratives that an increasing number of public figures promote in different European countries. Such an approach, as explained by Bounia, can also increase awareness about the bonds of solidarity that can be created between host communities and (im)migrants. Becoming institutions without walls will certainly help museums to redefine themselves and have a greater role in social change.

Of course, solidarity with and hospitality towards (im)migrants and refugees are necessary, especially for individuals who have just arrived in a host country. However, this is far from enough. Indeed, solidarity and charity establish power relations, rather than being benign actions. In the words of Mauss, "the unreciprocated gift still makes the person who has accepted it inferior, particularly when it has been accepted with no thought of returning it."[3] The image of refugees and migrants as targets for charity perpetuates the dichotomy of us/European citizens versus the (im)migrants/ the Other. Hence the importance of the idea of the "capacity to aspire" developed by Arjun Appadurai,[4] used here in Catalani's chapter and found as a recurring theme throughout the volume. The capacity to aspire is the ability of a person to use her culture and past as resources to create a better future for herself. This idea is quite close to the understanding of one's culture and heritage as part of a capability set that includes the different tools and skills possessed by individuals to achieve what they want to be and do.[5] The "capacity to aspire" or "capability approach" are important in redefining (im)migrants and refugees as having the same aspirations as any other citizen. Colomer's and Catalani's chapters detail how personal heritage and culture help people to navigate through change and give them a sense of personal direction, resilience, courage, and a way of envisioning the future(s).

My own research has clarified how heritage and culture can be essential in helping (im)migrants and refugees to learn the language of the host country and to acquire employable skills. The intensive work I have conducted with immigrant populations in Denmark, England, and France has revealed that learning the language of the host country and getting some form of employment are their two major preoccupations. These skills are, as far as I am concerned, essential for these individuals to create a better

---

3 Mauss, *The Gift*, 85.
4 Appadurai, *Future as Cultural Fact.*
5 Sen, "Capability and Well-Being," 277.

future and to exercise their capacity to aspire. Of course, it is important to discuss the cultural identity and heritage of immigrants, but it is also essential to find ways in which cultural institutions in the host country can assist these individuals in realizing what they want to be and do. This is, for me, the only way in which refugees and (im)migrants will be considered equal to any other European citizen and will stop being seen as the exoticized Other. My research details that museums have a key role to play in providing opportunities for immigrants to learn the language of their host country and to gain employment skills.[6]

The chapter by Feliu-Torruella and colleagues is particularly relevant at a time when discriminatory practices and racism in education have been denounced in several countries. This has included unfair grading for students from ethnic minorities, predominantly white curricula, and a lack of opportunities for minority teachers and researchers. The chapter demonstrates the need for greater integration of heritage (both tangible and intangible) in citizenship and multicultural education from a very young age. It is only through such a radical change of mind-sets, starting from the youngest age, that discrimination and racism can be efficiently combatted. Most importantly, introducing young children to multicultural heritage from different periods can help to deconstruct the widely held belief (for example, in the Brexit campaign) that migration is a recent phenomenon in most countries. However, recent research has revealed how heritage-based teaching currently reinforces an exclusionary approach to ethnic identity (Goodwin, in prep.). This exclusionary construction of ethnic identity has been explained in Clopot's chapter on the Russian Old Believers in Romania. Groups still build their identities on difference and uniqueness around their heritage in order to maintain an us/them dichotomy. As Clopot explains, this happens for both majority and minority ethnic groups and might relate to the (unfounded) fear of one's own heritage and culture disappearing if diversity and external influences are better taken into account in the construction of individual and collective identities. The chapter demonstrates that efforts still need to be made to construct alternative understandings of heritage and identities that are inclusive of external influences and that can be used for multicultural education and to fight against racism and discrimination.

Considering these bleak uses of heritage for exclusionary identity construction, Brandellero's chapter explains that "world music" has the power to create hybrid forms of heritage and culture, and can be used to teach tolerance and multiculturalism. For instance, when I worked for the Grenoble Jazz Festival (France) in 1995, we organized masterclasses in schools with the Afro-Americans David Murray and David Irving III and the Senegalese Doudou Ndiaye Rose. Students from different music schools had the opportunity to learn to play some of the tracks from Murray's album *Fo Deuk Revue* (1997). However, as Brandellero admits, world music is a niche and overshadowed by Western and commercial pop music. In addition, multicultural music projects like the one I coordinated have been massively cut during the recent public funding crisis.

6 Labadi, *Museums, Immigrants, and Social Justice.*

I would like to finish with the need for self-awareness and criticism of widely accepted notions. The authors of this book have carefully used the term "refugee crisis." This phrase was defined in Bounia's chapter as "a rather Eurocentric way to describe the increased movement of refugees mainly from Syria, but also from other countries, such as Afghanistan and Iraq, to Europe via the Greek islands and Italy, over the summer of 2015 and the first few months of 2016." I have always been wary of this phrase, not so much for its Eurocentric dimension as for its distortion of reality. The latest migratory wave is undeniably the biggest of the past thirty years, but the figures should be put into context. The majority of refugees or asylum seekers do not come to Europe. In 2015, out of the 60 million refugees or asylum seekers in the world, only 4 million came to Europe. Not a single European country is in the top ten that welcome the most refugees or asylum seekers. These people tend to go to neighbouring countries, as is the case, for instance, with 95 percent of all Syrian refugees.[7] For me, the current migratory phenomena are not a crisis in Europe because of the relatively small number of refugees and asylum seekers hosted there (although some countries are more impacted by these phenomena than others, for instance Greece, Italy, and Spain as often the first point of arrival of refugees and asylum seekers, but not their final destination). The use of the word "crisis" in this context therefore indicates more a political transformation and reappropriation of reality than the truth. The word is also used to hide a lack of political willingness to apply the basic values of the European Union: respect for human dignity, freedom, equality, nondiscrimination, tolerance, solidarity, and human rights. As researchers, we need to do more to question and contest these biased, political, and Eurocentric accounts of migratory phenomena.

Bibliography

Appadurai, Arjun, *The Future as Cultural Fact: Essays on the Global Condition*. London: Verso, 2013.

Baynham, Mike, Celia Roberts, Melanie Cooke, James Simpson, Katerina Ananiadou, John Callaghan, James McGoldrick, and Catherina Wallace. *Effective Teaching and Learning: ESOL*, London: NRDC, 2007.

Fleury, Benjamin. 2015. "La plupart des migrants ne se réfugient pas en Europe." *La Tribune de Genève*. September 3, 2015. Available from: https://m.tdg.ch/articles/23654813. Accessed April 16, 2019.

Goodwin, Karl. "Ancient Culture and Modern Ethnicity: Exploring the Politics behind Recreations of Roman Cultural Identity in Museums and Heritage Displays." Unpublished PhD diss. University of Kent, in preparation.

Labadi, Sophia. *Museums, Immigrants, and Social Justice*. London:: Routledge, 2017.

——. "The National Museum of the Immigration History (Paris; France): Neo-colonialist Representations, Silencing, and Re-appropriation." *Journal of Social Archaeology* 13 (2013): 310–33.

Mauss, Marcel. *The Gift* [1950]. London: Routledge, 2002.

Sen, Amartya. "Capability and Well-Being." In *The Philosophy of Economics: An Anthology*. Edited by D. H. Hausman, 270–94. 3rd ed. Cambridge: Cambridge University Press, 2007.

---

7 Fleury, "La plupart des migrants."

Sophia Labadi is Professor in Heritage at the University of Kent. She is also a Leadership Fellow of the Arts and Humanities Research Council (United Kingdom) for research on Rethinking Heritage for Development (2019–2020). Sophia is the author of more than sixty publications, including *Museums, Immigrants, and Social Justice* (2017), *UNESCO, Cultural Heritage and Outstanding Universal Value* (2013), Heritage and Globalisation (2010, coedited with Colin Long), and *The Cultural Turn in International Aid* (2019) (School of European Culture and Languages, University of Kent, United Kingdom; email: s.labadi@kent.ac.uk).

INDEX

"n" indicates a footnote that adds to the information in the text; the ensuing numeral indicates the number of the footnote; "ill" indicates an illustration.

"actants," 83, 89, 92, 94
affects/affectivity, 48–49, 84–85, 84n11, 86, 89–90, 91, 92–93, 94, 104
affective materialities, 84, 93, 94
alba KULTUR, 104
artifacts/antiquities, 25, 32, 43, 59, 83
aspiration *see* "capacity to aspire"
asylum seekers, 12, 27, 30, 31, 114
    see also displaced individuals;
        migrants; refugees

"Balkan route," 40, 47
belonging, sense/feeling of, 18, 19, 20, 21, 28, 32, 36, 56, 64
    cultural, 11–12, 16
    social/community, 1, 2, 73, 85, 93
border controls/closures, 31, 40
Brexit, 113

"capability approach," 112
"capacity to aspire," 11, 15, 21, 112–13
coexistence/cohabitation, 54, 55–56, 85, 108
coloniality, 32–33, 55
    cultural robbery, 25–26
    see also postcoloniality
commonality, 44–46, 79
community (as museum concept), 34–35, 36
cosmopolitanism, 1, 102
Council of Europe, 55
    "Cultural Heritage and Its Educational Implications" (1995), 54
    European Democratic Citizenship (Tim Copeland, 2006), 54, 56, 65
    Framework Convention for the Protection of National Minorities (1995), 70

Framework Convention on the Value of Cultural Heritage for Society (Faro, 2005), 54, 65
    Recommendation of the Committee of Ministers (1998), 53
creative strategies, 29
cultural rights/appropriation, 54, 55, 56, 100–101

dance, 26, 32, 35
diasporas, 2, 39, 71, 72, 73, 89, 94
Dirty Pretty Things (Stephen Frears), 30
displaced individuals, 1–2, 11–21
    Afghani, 17n26, 19–20, 40 and n. 5, 114
    Congolese, 12, 14, 17n26, 25, 31–32
    Iranian, 33, 40
    Iraqi, 3, 40 and n. 5, 114
    "Living Ghosts," 30
    longing, 13, 14, 18, 19
    as newcomers/"guests," 3, 11, 13, 30, 39, 112
    Pakistani, 3, 40
    possessions/objects/garments, 30, 33, 35, 39, 43, 83–94, 88ill, 90ill, 92ill
    Rhaidesti (Bisanthean), 43
    sea crossings
        Aegean, 40
        English Channel, 31
    Senegalese, 3, 113
    Somali, 40, 87
    Syrian, 12, 16–17 and n. 24, 19, 40 and n. 47, 114
    Thai, 99
    Ugandan, 99
    see also asylum seekers migrants; refugees
displacement, 11–18, 21
    forced, 87–88

displacement (*cont.*)
  levels of, 1–2
  see also displaced individuals
diversity, 28, 46, 48, 54, 57–59, 59n17,
  94, 102, 103–5
  cultural, 55–56, 70, 79
  "superdiversity," 99, 101–2, 104–5,
    108, 111–14
  "united in diversity," 69

education *see* heritage: education; New
    Education movement
emotions, 84–87, 89–90, 91, 92–93
En Chordais, Greece, 107
"entanglement," 83–85, 86–87, 91, 93
"ethics of care," 40, 42–44, 46, 48–49
Europe *see* host communities
European Union, 3, 69–70, 114
  post-socialist countries, 69
  Turkey agreement (2016), 40, 43
Europeanization, 69, 70, 79

ghostly metaphor, 33–34; *see also*
    displaced individuals: "Living
    Ghosts"; spectrality
"global ethnoscapes," 2
globalization, 2, 3, 69–70, 72, 79; *see also*
    Europeanization
"glocality," 1, 2
governance *see* host communities:
    Europe
Greek islands, 30, 40 and n. 5, 47, 114
Grenoble Jazz Festival, 113

heritage
  absence/death of, 3, 11, 12,
    13–14, 16, 20
  "absence–presence," 13–15, 16, 18, 20,
    21, 30, 31, 32, 85, 86
  Authorized Heritage Discourse (AHD),
    28, 101
  education, 53–65, 113
    Historic Schools of Barcelona,
      56–65, 58ill, 59n17,
      61ill, 63ill
      architecture of, 57, 60–62, 62n25

    history of, 57
    see also practices: education
  memory, 59, 65
  progressive pedagogy, 59, 60
  systematic observation method, 60
  "meaning making," 100
  music, 25, 99–108
    folk/local traditions, 99, 103, 106,
      107, 108
    memory of, 99, 108
    programmers, 1, 99–100, 102–8
    "world music," 99–100, 102–8, 113
    see also alba KULTUR; En Chordais;
      Grenoble Jazz Festival;
      practices; WOMAD
  overcoming hardship, as a means of,
    16–18, 19, 20
  ownership, 32, 36, 89, 100, 107
  as performance, 28, 99, 102
  Performing Heritage (Jackson &
    Kidd), 29
  resilience of, 11–12, 14–15, 16–18,
    21, 112
  revaluation of, 2–3, 11, 12, 14, 15,
    18, 20, 21
  shared, 11, 13–18, 20, 56–57, 60, 64,
    65, 105
  tangible/intangible, 18n28, 21, 39, 56,
    59, 73, 94, 100, 113
    intangible cultural heritage (ICH),
      11, 13–14, 15–16, 73, 75–79,
      99, 103, 105–6, 107
  tourism, 15, 59, 90
Hiroshima, paper cranes of, 33
homing processes, 85, 86, 93
host/local communities, 12–13, 13n9,
    18, 27, 36, 41, 42
  Denmark, 77, 102, 112
  donations, 44, 46
  Europe (generally), 2–3, 11, 16–17,
    21, 40–41, 104, 105,
    108, 111–14
    Central, 69, 103
    Eastern, 3, 69
    governance of, 69
    Northern, 3, 40, 55
    Southern, 3

Western (and the West generally), 3, 55, 57, 65, 102, 113
  see also "Balkan route"; European Union
France, 16, 102, 112
Germany, 99, 102, 103
Greece/Greeks, 40, 44–46, 49, 102, 103, 107, 112, 114
  Athens, 40, 43, 46
  Thessaloniki, 48
Italy, 40n5, 77, 78, 102, 114
outside Europe, 114
Romania/Romanian Old Believers, 70–79, 71n28, 74ill, 113
  Community of Lipovan Russians in Romania (CRLR), 72, 75
  history, 70–72, 72n34
  language, 75–78, 76ill
  rituals/beliefs/ceremonies, 73–75, 74n49, 77–78
Slovakia, 99, 102, 103
  World Music Festival Bratislava, 103 and n. 30
Spain, 77, 78, 114
Sweden, 87
United Kingdom, 12, 16, 19, 25, 26, 77, 102
  England, 112
  London, 30, 91
  Manchester, 12–13, 25–36
  Community Arts North West (CAN), 26 and n. 2
humanitarianism see nongovernmental organizations; workers

ICH see heritage: intangible cultural heritage
identity, 19, 26–28, 59, 60, 70, 73, 87–88, 100–101, 107, 113
  collective, 56, 64, 113
  (re)construction of, 28, 54, 65, 84, 89, 93–94, 100–102, 113
  contingent, 27, 29–36, 72–73, 93
  cultural, 1–3, 17, 20, 21, 56, 69, 88, 93, 94, 111
  reassertion of, 13
  redefinition, 14, 15, 17, 21

resistant, 72–73, 78–79;
  "sedimentary identities," 105
  see also refugees
India, 15
integration, 2, 21, 39, 55, 69–70

Julian calendar, 73–74

language, 13n9, 55, 73, 112–13
  creolization, 2, 102
  see also host communities: Romania/ Romanian Old Believers

magic, 25
materiality, 13–14, 20, 31, 46, 59, 72, 83–94
memory/memories, 14, 17, 19–21, 20n38, 39, 41, 84–85, 89–94, 103, 107
  absence of, 12
  collective/shared/social, 14, 20, 33, 84
  as comfort, 16, 19
  constructed, 20, 87, 91
  selective/inaccurate, 14 and n. 18, 15, 20, 29, 102
  see also heritage: education; heritage: music
migrants/immigrants/migration, 2–3, 12, 26, 30, 55, 77, 79, 84–95, 111–14
  economic, 2
  en masse, 28
  forced, 2, 3, 11, 12–16, 16–17n24, 18, 20, 21, 87
  internal, 3
  multiple, 86
  transnational, 85, 86, 87, 89
  see also asylum seekers; displaced individuals; heritage: education; heritage: music; host communities: Romania/ Romanian Old Believers; museums; refugees
mobility, 3, 70, 72, 84, 85, 86, 91, 92–93, 94
  artistic, 106
multiculturalism, 3, 21, 28, 54–56, 65, 69, 87, 101, 105, 113

museums, 3, 25–36, 39–49, 84, 94–95,
    111, 113
    as activists or as historians, 41–44, 48,
        49, 111
    Athens exhibitions, 40, 43,
        44–46, 48–49
    "A Museum without a Home"
        (Amnesty International/Oxfam), 43,
        44–46, 45ill, 112
        Belgrade (Mikser
            Festival—Migration), 44
        Glasgow (Refugee Festival
            Scotand), 44
        Ioannina (Exhibition of
            Hospitality), 43, 44
        New York (72nd United National
            General Assembly), 44
    Barcelona History Museum, 62
    Manchester, 25–36, 111
        Ancient Worlds Galleries, 35
        Egyptian Worlds Gallery, 33
        Living Cultures Gallery, 25, 31–32
        theatre, 25–36, 35n51, 111
            Flying Carpets, 25–27, 26n2, 26n4,
                29, 34–35
            interactivity, 28–29, 31, 32, 35
            Samedi Soir, 25, 31, 32, 35
    Mytilene exhibitions, 43
    Paris Musée National de l'Histoire de
        l'Immigration, 111
    Thessaloniki exhibitions, 40,
        43, 47–49
        Archaeological Museum, 43
        Museum of Photography, 43, 47
    see also practices: museum
music see heritage: music
mythical figures/superstitions,
        25–26, 33, 35 see also host
        communities: Romania/
        Romanian Old Believers

Network of European Museum
    Organizations (NEMO), 43
"network society," 72
New Education movement, 57, 60, 62
nongovernmental organizations
        (NGOs), 40–41, 42, 43–44,
        46, 49, 72

Old Believers see host communities:
    Romania/Romanian Old
    Believers

postcoloniality, 1, 2 see also coloniality
practices
    cultural, 11, 12, 14, 18, 19, 100, 106, 107
    education, 65, 113
    embodied, 21
    heritage, 11, 16, 18, 20–21, 28, 35,
        73–75, 87, 99, 100
        intangible cultural heritage
            (ICH), 79
        museum, 35, 41, 43, 48, 49, 94
        music, 99–100, 102, 103, 104, 106,
            107, 108
    of placeness, 85
    religious, 73–75, 77
    social, 32, 72
    traditional, 18, 77

racism, 113
refugees, 2, 11–21, 28, 30–31, 42, 44–46,
        87–88, 112–14
    artists, 25–27, 26n2, 29, 31, 32,
        33–36, 111
    "community," 12, 16–17, 18, 34–35
    "crisis," 2, 39–41, 40n5, 43, 47–49, 114
    identity, 27
    Pepper's Ghost (analogous theatrical
        device), 31
    restrictions in home countries, 34
    see also asylum seekers displaced
        individuals migrants
Russian Orthodox Church, 71–72, 75

Sámi (Laplanders), 78
social media, 2, 47, 103
    "The Archaeology of a Mobile
        Life" Facebook status,
        85–94, 86n19
solidarity, 1, 42, 44, 46, 47, 48, 73,
        112, 114
    "solidarity cities," 17n25
spatiality, 30, 31
spectrality, 30, 32, 34–35 see also
        displaced individuals "Living
        Ghosts"

stories, 11, 12, 14 and n. 18, 18, 19, 21,
33, 39, 85, 88–89
storytellers/oral tradition, 25, 32,
103, 107

transit camps, Greece
Idomeni, 40, 47
Thessaloniki, 47
"travelling objects" (salvaged), 83–94,
88ill, 90ill, 92ill; *see also*
displaced individuals:
possessions

United Nations
Educational, Scientific and Cultural
Organization (UNESCO),
28, 106
High Commissioner for Refugees
(UNHCR), 1–2, 40–41
see also museums: New York
"unwanted," feeling of being, 18

workers, humanitarian, 41
World of Music, Arts and Dance
(WOMAD), 106